SUPER KIDS

Over 200 incredible ways for kids to

SAVE THE PLANET

Sasha Norris and Rupert Davies

THINK

First published in Great Britain in 2005 by Think Books
Think Publishing, The Pall Mall Deposit, 124 – 128 Barlby Road, London W10 6BL
www.thinkpublishing.co.uk

Author: Sasha Norris
Illustrator: Rupert Davies
Designer: Dominic Scott
Editor: Malcolm Tait
Assistant editors: Tania Adams and Sonja Patel

Norwich Union
Aviva plc, Registered in England 02468686
Registered office: St Helen's, 1 Undershaft, London EC3P 3DG
www.norwichunion.com

**NORWICH
UNION**
an **AVIVA** company

ISBN 1-84525-001-X

Printed and bound in Great Britain on 100% recycled paper, by Cambridge Printing.

A GREAT BIG SUPER THANK YOU

Super Kids everywhere would like to thank Norwich Union
for their support in putting together this book.
We couldn't have done it without them.
We're also very grateful to YPTE (Young People's Trust
for the Environment) and Wildlife Watch (The Wildlife
Trusts' club for younger members), who allowed us
to trawl through their fantastic info for our research.
Find out more about all these great
organisations at the back of this book.
Many thanks also to Nancy Gladstone of
Siren, for her invaluable research.
And for their support throughout, grateful thanks to
Josh Dugdale, Lynn Norris . . . and Lily.

Ready to become a Super Kid?

Super Kids, we're in a pickle. Adults and let's face it, most of them are Zombies – have been spending the last couple of centuries completely messing up the planet. If we continue to leave them in charge, it's only going to get worse. As this book shows, everything the Zombie Adults touch seems to be going wrong. Well, there's only one answer . . .

Your mission is to take charge and SAVE THE PLANET! The Zombie Adults are all around you – your Mum, Dad and teachers – and it's up to you to wake them up and make a difference!

So how do you become a Super Kid? If you're reading this, you're already on your way. You just need to make sure you read on! This little book is every Super Kid's bible – packed full of tips on how to save the planet and make a difference. If you're thinking it's just another boring, factual, school-type textbook, then think again. Super Kids is all about DOING! Every page is bursting with things to do, stuff to make, clubs to join and ways to help. What's more you'll be learning without realising it – this is learning made fun!

By the time you've finished this book, your head will be full of amazing SUPERFACTS to impress your friends and family with – perfect ammunition to quote at the Zombie Adults and wake them up! Want to tell your parents or teacher off for a change? Award them with the CERTIFICATE OF SHAME at the back of the book. They have to display it for all to see until they can prove they've changed their ways!

If you want to see how YOU score on an eco-friendly scale, check out the final section and see if you pass the Super Kids challenge!

START TODAY! START NOW! The planet is crying out for the Super Kids' mission to start. Its precious resources are being run dry by greedy humans. We rely on the earth for so many things and take them for granted.

Right this moment, you are holding in your hands one of these precious resources — paper. This amazing stuff, that we take for granted every day, is basically squashed trees. Many of the world's rainforests and animals are in danger, because of all the trees we're chopping down to make paper.

This book is printed on paper with a difference though. It's been 100% recycled (collected by fellow eco-heros, sent to a special recycling plant and made back into paper again) and de-inked (to remove any dye that was in the original paper, without nasty bleaching). You can see and feel that the paper is still good quality though — especially because it's got so many interesting and important things to say! It's also been coated in silk, another natural resource, to leave it smooth and shiny, so it's easy to read.

SUPERFACT
The average UK family uses six trees' worth of paper every year.

Being CarbonNeutral
This book will show you how decisions we make all have an effect on the environment. But to get this book to you, and arm you with all these ideas to help save the planet, a lot of energy has been used to write, print and get the book to the place you bought it.

In true Super Kids style we've done the sums and, with the help of Future Forests, worked out how much carbon dioxide, the primary contributor to  global warming, the book has created. We have then helped to plant trees that will absorb these emissions as they grow to maturity. These trees have been planted so you've got all the information you need to start your mission to save the planet without us making the problems worse before you've even got started. Future Forests was set up to make it easy and enjoyable for everyone to take positive action on climate change. Since Future Forests started in 1997, over 50,000 people and 200 businesses have become involved.

What's inside

8 Energy You may be full of it, Super Kids, but the planet is running out. Energy has to come from somewhere, and we've been getting it from all the wrong places. Here's your chance to be a bright spark.

24 Water We all need water to live, but some of us are using too much of it. Don't be a drip – read these pages and find out how to cut down on what you need.

36 Waste What happens to something when you chuck it away? It fills up the ground for centuries and centuries, killing off animals and plants. Find out all about the rubbish way we treat our planet.

48 Food You are what you eat, goes the old saying. Well, that's a bit worrying when you look at the rotten old stuff we fill our mouths with. Feast your eyes here on some great alternatives.

66 Home and School It's amazing what a mess those Zombie Adults make of the world. Your parents and teachers really need sorting out. It's time to bring the message home to them.

80 Pets Dogs and cats may be our best friends, but do we treat them that way? Do we really think about what we're doing to animals when they come and live with us? Here are some pet peeves.

Energy

OK, here we go eco-warriors. One of your main tasks is about to be revealed. Stand by. It's not going to be easy. The adults all around you — who pretend to know what they are doing — have made a major boo-boo. Things are going seriously wrong. We never thought that by innocently burning a bit of coal, we'd alter the planet forever.

To find out why, let's go back a few centuries, when life was very different. There was never anything very good on the telly — because the telly hadn't been invented yet. If you wanted to go out in the evening, there weren't any cars, buses or trains to take you — so you could only get as far as your legs would carry you. And you'd be walking in the dark, too — no street-lighting in those days. Fancy a meal? Better get the firewood together because microwaves haven't made it into the shops yet. And make sure there's enough wood for your heating too.

Yes, life was very different back then. So, being the brilliant humans we are, we changed it. We made machines, which burned oil, gas, and coal. These, we found tucked away in corners of the world where they'd been hiding for thousands of years. Now we can jump in the car, go where we like, heat our houses, make electric light, watch TV — and all by using fossil fuels dug out of the ground.

But here's the problem — the world is running out of them. And here's the second problem. The more we use them, the more we destroy the world.

Fossil fuels are literally made of fossils – the dead bodies of trees which fell down back in the swampy Carboniferous Period (360 to 286 million years ago) and were weighed down under the dead bodies of more trees and mud. They were squashed and squashed together, until millions of year later they became coal. Oil and natural gas are super-squidged layers of marine plankton, tiny creatures which float about in the ocean before landing up on the seafloor. Life – trees, plankton and you, Super Kids – is basically composed of carbon. And when you burn carbon in air, what do you get? Heat, water vapour and carbon dioxide. With the faithful combustion engine, we can turn that heat into motion and whizz off in our cars. With steam turbines in power stations, we can make electrical power and send it down power lines to light our houses and heat our bathwater. Meanwhile, the carbon dioxide just kind of hangs around.

Having some of this carbon dioxide in the atmosphere is a good thing, because it keeps the heat in, like panes of glass in a greenhouse. If it wasn't for gases like carbon dioxide, we'd all be chilling out at -18°C. But the more we keep burning fossil fuels, the more 'greenhouse gases' are building up in our atmosphere. And the result? Global warming. Unfortunately, we're not talking about sunning yourself on your patio in December. Climate change means more weird, spooky, mad and wild weather, which is unpredictable and can kill people. It means droughts, heatwaves, floods and cyclones – and it's the people in the poorest countries, who have only just started to burn fossil fuels, that will suffer the most. It's so unfair!

And there you have it – that's how the combustion of fossil fuels, the most brilliant of all human inventions could end up destroying our own planet. But fear not, 'cos that's where you come in, Super Kids! These fossil fuels are going to run out one day, anyway.

Even if it wasn't for global warming, we need alternatives. And we need them fast.

Join the energy detectives

Right Sherlock. Time to do some detective work on those Zombie Parents! Get them to take a few moments to sit down and answer some questions on the following website: http://www.bestfootforward.com/footprintlife.htm. This is the ultimate detective tool. It calculates how eco-friendly their lifestyle is by working out their 'carbon footprint.' The more carbon they use, the bigger their footprint, the more they are contributing to climate change. How big are your parents feet?!

Fill the kettle half-full

Making Zombie Mum a cup of fairtrade tea? Only fill the kettle with as much water as you need. Now if you really want to spoil her, you'll do the washing up too. Just make sure you put a plug in the sink. Leaving the hot tap running is literally throwing money – and the planet – down the drain.

Switch on to switching off

You know that little red light on the front of the telly, the one that means you don't have to get up to turn it off? Well, lazy bones – get up and turn it off! Leaving things like TVs, computers and hi-fi equipment on stand-by takes up 1% of all the electricity used in the UK. Leaving your mobile phone charger switched on at the wall, when you're not charging your phone, uses up energy too. As does leaving lights on when no-one is in the room. Make sure you flick that switch on the way out!

Heat just as much water as you need in your
kettle – if there's some left over, see if you can
use it for something else.

Fridges may look innocent but . . .

Fridges sit in the corner of the kitchen, humming quietly to themselves, but are they guzzling more energy than needed to keep your food fresh? If you put hot food in the fridge, the poor thing has to work harder to cool it down. This uses up even more energy. And if you follow the power lines from the plug in your kitchen to the power station, it ends up squirting more carbon dioxide into the atmosphere, too. The back of the fridge is where all the hard work of cooling down inside the fridge is done. If there's fluff on the coils, it will be less efficient – more electricity is needed to cool your food. So Super Kids, keep it clean to keep it green!

Washing the eco-way

Who does the washing in your house? Check that they fill the washing machine as full as possible, use the lowest temperature setting possible, and then hang clothes out to dry using the amazing power of the sun and wind. Don't tumble-dry them, which uses up more fossil fuels!

Shut up!

Some like it hot, so shut the curtains to stop that precious heat escaping. If your heating is on when no-one's home, or if it's simply too tropical, don't open the window. Get someone to turn the heating off or lower the temperature on the thermostat.

Who does the washing in your house? Check that they
fill the washing machine as full as possible.

Do-It-Yourself home climate care

Anyone in your family keen on DIY? Here are a couple of energy-saving jobs for them. If they seem a bit reluctant to get up off the sofa, just remind them that saving energy = saving money = saving the planet. Get to work on the radiators first. Put shelves above and reflective foil behind them, so all that valuable heat energy is sent out into the room.

Next, eco-heroes, agitate to insulate! Get your DIY expert to fill in any gaps where draughts get in. You could even get them to buy a cute little jacket for the boiler, which keeps the water hotter for longer and uses less energy.

Look for the logo

Thought only school kids got grades? In fact boilers, fridges or anything that uses electricity does too. Have a look at electrical equipment at home or school and find the European Energy Label. Appliances with grade A are the best — they cost less to run and save on carbon dioxide emissions. The very best electrical appliances will have an Energy Efficiency Recommended logo, awarded by the Energy Saving Trust. See www.saveenergy.co.uk for more ways to save energy in your home.

Check for the Energy Efficiency Recommended logo on all the electrical appliances you use.

Get on the sunny side

The sun is a huge ball of fire, a mass of energy, of material burning up in outer space nine million miles away. It's so far away that it takes eight minutes for light from the sun to reach us here on Earth. In the centre of the sun, it's 15,000,000°C and it's been burning for the last 4.6 billion years.

This solar energy is the power source of eco-heroes everywhere. You don't have to worry about the sun running out. It just sits in the sky, smiling down, offering humans the chance to POWER THE WHOLE WORLD. Yet all we can do is dig around in the middle of our planet for more fossil fuels to burn.

Why? Because you can't hold the sun in your hand, put it in a tin can or petrol pump, and people like to be able to sell things to make money. The good news is, more people are realising there's this huge ball of fire, for free. It can heat our water, warm our houses and cook our supper. You can even use solar power to recharge your batteries, your watch and even your mobile phone. Look for cool solar gadgets at www.solarenergyalliance.com and www.selectsolar.co.uk.

Get windy

Windy day? All that air rushing about can be put to good use. Like old-fashioned windmills, wind turbines take the power out of the wind and turn it into electricity.

So why not build your own windmill? Try a K'Nex kit, which is designed to piece together the different parts. Or use straws, which are a great alternative. To get started visit http://sln.fi.edu//tfi/units/energy/buildwindmill.html.

When your windmill is complete, try it out against an electric fan, and see wind converted to energy before your very eyes!

Once you start making your own windmills, it gets difficult to know when to stop!

Bio Power

Biomass is the sun's energy stored by life. It's the carbon that's found in every single plant and animal on the planet. Although it still produces carbon dioxide when it's burnt, as new plants and trees grow they absorb carbon dioxide from the atmosphere. It's a cycle.

This means that using biomass for energy, like burning wood, doesn't lead to the creation of extra carbon dioxide. It's good news for the climate, as long as new trees replace the old ones.

So don't forget – if you burn wood, plant a tree!

Burn poo!

Another way to get the energy out of biomass is by looking in some very smelly places. Burning the gas from animal poo like cowpats is a clever way to stop methane, a gas 21 times as bad for the climate as carbon dioxide, getting into the atmosphere – and it makes energy at the same time. Who'd have thought cowpats could be the energy of the future!

Renewable revolution

Solar, wind, biomass – these are all renewable sources of energy. That means there's always more to be had – unlike the fossil fuels. At the moment, only 3% of the UK's electricity comes from renewable sources. Your mission, should you choose to accept it, is to increase this miniscule proportion. Start by looking up The Energy Saving Trust at www.est.org.uk and Clear Skies at www.clear-skies.org, which help households and communities switch to renewable energy. Spread the word, Super Kids!

Every time you burn wood, plant a tree.

WORLD GONE MAD
WARNING: NUCLEAR POWER

Nuclear power, Super Kids, is a hi-tech way of making energy that's completely renewable. It involves breaking open the tiniest part of cells – through nuclear fission – inside massive machines called reactors. This is a process that can be repeated over and over again and does not require loads of materials like fossil fuels. But nuclear power has an evil side-effect . . .

Imagine, Super Kids, if you invented something that could attack the recipe by which all humans are made – our DNA. This is the stuff that tells a dog to have a waggy tail, a human to have a round head and walk on two legs, a scorpion to run around being scary and a cheetah to be fast. DNA is the code, the set of rules, the bottom line for every living thing.

Well it's stranger than fiction, Super Kids, weirder than the X files and Buffy – humans are now making nuclear energy from a process, which produces as its waste, radioactive material that messes around with our DNA.

It really is the stuff of nightmares Super Kids, because it takes thousands of years for this waste to become harmless. And meanwhile, it has to be stored somewhere.

Don't let them convince you that nuclear power is the answer, Super Kids. Campaign against it at www.cnd.org.

SUPERFACT
Radioactive sand has been found on Scottish islands from Sellafield nuclear power station. Some has been found as far away as Greenland, Norway and Northern Ireland.

Nuclear power has become the stuff of nightmares.

Sneaky bills

If the Zombie Parents insist that the installation of solar panels or a wind-turbine is not for them, sneak a peek at your electricity and gas bills. Who sells you the energy to power your super-hero home? If they haven't got a RENEWABLE ENERGY TARIFF, use all available methods of persuasion to get your parents to organise one.

This means the energy company supplies you with electricity from renewable sources. The more people with this kind of tariff, the more we will come to rely on renewables, instead of stinky fossil fuels or scary nuclear. Energy suppliers with good renewable tariffs include www.unit-e.co.uk, www.ecotricity.co.uk and www.nieenergy.co.uk.

Make bricks

If you have an open fire at home, you can buy a kit from the Centre for Alternative Energy (CAT) or Natural Collection to make bricks from newspaper. You soak your newspaper, squash it into the brick-maker and leave it to dry. The results burn for hours and manage to recycle, reuse and reduce all at once. See www.cat.org.uk or www.naturalcollection.com.

Get efficient

For the moment, almost all our energy comes from burning fossil fuels, so it makes sense to use as little energy as we can. That doesn't mean you get to laze about all day! Small changes, if we all make them, will add up to a huge energy saving. The less carbon dioxide in the atmosphere, the less risk of global warming!

The idea is to burn the old newspaper
bricks, not read them!

I t might not feel like it when you have to play games in the rain, but water is scarce! Yes really — only 2% of the water on this blue planet is fresh and not full of salt. We can't drink salty water — try a tiny drop and see. Yuk! We need the fresh stuff, and of that 2% only a very tiny amount is actually out there for us to drink. The rest is wrapped up in huge glaciers, like the one that bashed and sank the Titanic.

So where does your household water actually come from? We know water falls out of the sky as rain — but how does it get into your tap? Most areas have a local water 'source', usually a pool of water held in a river or reservoir. Your local water company takes this water, adds some chemicals to clean it, and then sends it to your home. Under the ground, through pipes in your street it comes, rushing and gurgling. If the water were not in your house, it would still be in the river or reservoir, where lots of animals live wet and slippery lives, and need the water to survive.

Most of the time there is enough water for everyone and everything. Sometimes though, a disaster can happen — there is a DROUGHT! This happens when there is not enough water to go around. Humans suffer when water levels are low — but remember, the animals do too. More water is used up than they can cope with losing, and they may even die.

So do we really need water that much? You see, we're virtually made of the stuff. If you could put a human in a liquidiser (don't try this at home!) and various parts of the body, like protein and fat, were sorted into test tubes, 80% of the stuff you got out would be WATER! Our bodies are just one big water bottle. Our skin is like a flask.

The same goes for most living creatures on the planet. We can't do anything without water, yet so often we treat it like it's worthless. Especially the Zombie Parents. They spend loads of time worrying about money and other stuff — but how much time do they spend thinking about the MOST PRECIOUS THING ON EARTH. Water! Remember, they can't help it. Their brains are stuck and it's up to us to change them.

Every day we willfully use and then chuck away over 150 litres of water — that's 150 of those big pop or water bottles. Why should it matter? Well, for a start its just unfair. Lots of people in the world, about one third in fact, don't have ANY clean water. Can you imagine going even a single day without water? (Don't try this at home, either!). People in countries like India and South Africa trek for hours to get water out of a well, and then bring it home in heavy containers to cook, wash and drink.

Secondly, water in the tap doesn't come free. It costs energy and money to make it clean enough to drink, and that damages the planet too.

Finally, water is essential to all life on earth — not just humans. If we waste it, we are wasting it for everyone and everything.

Think about every drop you use and be wise with water.

Do the tap dance

You go to the sink, you grab your toothpaste, turn on the tap to wet your brush – and being a global warrior, on a mission to save the planet, you turn it back off again as you brush! Then, when you need to wet the brush again, turn it back on, then off again. On, off, on off! Get a rhythm going. You can save 4.5 litres of water every time you polish your pegs, if you just remember the tap dance.

SUPERFACT

Remember to turn every tap off properly when you finish with it. If every household in the country left one tap dripping, the country would lose an amazing 750 million litres of water, every single day!

Bricking it!

Of course, not everyone feels comfortable about not flushing, so here's a sneaky way to minimise the amount of water you flush away. Every time you pull that lever, you're emptying the cistern – that box at the back of the loo – of all the water it holds. A good flush doesn't need as much water as most cisterns hold. So, wouldn't it be great if there was a way to make the cistern hold less? Well, there is. Simply put a brick in it, and every time the cistern refills after a flush, the brick takes up some of the space, saving water every time!

Do you really need to flush?

You stumble out of bed and into the loo – ah, that's a relief! Time to flush away the liquid you've just discharged. Or is it? A massive one third of the water we use every day is from flushing the loo. Now, clearly, there are times when you have to flush, but is it really necessary every time?

Here's the golden rule for all Super Kids: 'If its yellow, let it mellow, if its brown, flush it down!'

Put a brick in your cistern. Every time someone flushes, you'll save the planet a brick's worth of water. Over a year, you'll have saved enough water to fill a room!

Join the SAS

No, not the armed forces, Surfers Against Sewage – they've got to be the coolest eco-group out there! These surfers decided that swimming around in poo was really grim, so they formed a group to do something about it.

Poo ends up in the sea when sewage is pumped in directly through long pipes. Thank goodness this doesn't happen in Britain anymore! That's all thanks to eco-warriors just like you, who have lobbied for change. The Surfers Against Sewage also set up a conservation organisation to look after our beaches and oceans. If you live in the right areas, they will take you surfing, then teach you how to look after the sea! See www.sas.org.uk.

Take a power shower

I bet you never thought taking a shower would help you save the world, but wait until you see the facts. The average bath uses 80 litres of water, while the average shower only uses 40. Half the water means half the eco-disaster. You could make the figure even less, by showering as quickly as you can.

Hold on a minute Super Kids. In that case, do you really need to wash at all? Hmm – here comes mum!

What's at the bottom of your garden?

If you want to be a really radical eco-warrior and run the risk of waking up the Zombie Parents forever, put a bale of straw in your garden and pee on that. OK, slightly easier for male eco-warriors, than female ones! If your Dad or your nosy neighbour asks what you're doing, tell them you're saving the world. If this is not enough for them, tell them the straw absorbs the nitrogenous waste in your urine, turning it into perfect compost for the garden. It also reduces the amount of sewage dealt with by the water authorities. If that's not enough, show them this book!

Hooray, here come the **SAS**.
That's the **Surfers Against Sewage!**

Be a supersnoop and report eco-crime

Have you seen dead fish floating on the river? Maybe the water is discoloured and smelly? Fertiliser, industrial waste, oil or the effect of global warming or industrial heating on the water, may be the cause. All incidents of river pollution should be reported to the Pollution Control officer at the Water Authority. Give as much detail as you can – the date, time, exact place and precisely what you saw. Occasionally, poisonous substances are deliberately dumped into rivers. This is called 'fly-tipping'. If you see this going on, take the registration number of the vehicle and if possible, get the name of the firm. This is a matter for the police!

Waste not, want not

A really brilliant way to save water is to use it more than once. It's so simple!

SUPERFACT

In 1992, there were 611 incidents of oil pollution in UK coastal waters alone!

If you really must have a bath, the water you leave behind might not be anything you'd fancy drinking, but the plants in your garden probably wouldn't say no to a sip or two – as long as you haven't used chemical-ridden bath foam or oils. Simply top up a watering can with your old bath-water, and give your garden a good dunking, too!

Save water on holiday

Eco-heroes can't afford to rest (too much!), on holiday. While you're idling, you may be adding to local global eco-disasters. Perhaps your Mum likes to take two showers a day when she's in Spain, soaking up the sun? In fact, Spain often doesn't have enough water for its own people, never mind us smelly Brits wallowing in it. Tell your mum to wear a bit more of that eco-deodorant and swim in the sea. If she really needs to have a wash, tell her to make the shower quick. It might feel relaxing standing under there for hours, but not if you think of the terrapins parched in their ponds. It's murder for them!

Reuse bath-water whenever you can – but make sure
others are finished with it first!

Love your river

Become friends with the animals which share your water source. Visit your local reservoir with your Zombie Parents – take a pair of binoculars to see what you can see. Why not:

● Try and spot six different species of ducks. Take a guide book to help you.

● Look out for otters, herons, terns and gulls, which also live down on the river.

● Remember Ratty from *Wind in the Willows*? See if you can find him. He's actually a water vole, now a rare sight in British rivers.

● Take a net and jam-jar to your local river. Fish about in the shallows for sticklebacks and minnows. IMPORTANT! Always put creatures back after you've had a good marvel at them.

The better you know about the animals you're helping, Super Kids, the more they'll become a real part of your life.

Never pour oil down the drain!

When your mum's been cooking, what does she do with the left-over oil? If she pours it down the sink, STOP HER! Scientists have shown that most oil that ends up polluting the sea comes from humans dumping it down the drain. Even a few litres of oil spilled in a lake can produce a thin film over thousands of square metres and kill plants and animals! The 380,000 tonnes of oil illegally poured down drains could have been disposed of without any harm to the environment. Tell Mum to wait until oils and fats have cooled and solidified. Now she can put them in the bin, where they can be soaked into household rubbish. Some councils even collect vegetable oils and recycle them.

Dad can do his bit to stop oil pollution too. Any old oil that's been used in the car or on a bicycle can be recycled at the oil bank. Not sure where this is? Find one near to you at www.oilbankline.org.uk.

Get to know your local stream well – it's amazing what you can find.

Choose tap water

All Super Kids need to have a bottle of water (or as scientists say, H_2O) on them, to keep them going through the day. Remember you should be drinking two litres a day. Buying mineral water is healthy, but next time you've finished with the bottle, don't chuck it away.

Simply fill it up with tap water – it's fine to drink and it's free. Reuse it for a few weeks before you buy a new one.

Support Water Aid

Ok Super Kids, its time to get serious. Stare into your Super Kids' looking glass and get some global perspective on water in the wider world. Look at Africa, India or Indonesia – there you will see people suffering terrible diseases, thirsty and hungry, unable to grow food or even drink a simple glass of clean water. One child dies, somewhere in the world every 15 seconds, because they do not have something as simple as clean water! But there are people trying to help, making wells and water purification systems (to clean the water). They, like you, are global-heroes for change. Their work means that kids can survive. Be global Super Kids and help them – visit www.wateraid.co.uk.

Butt in!

Here's a great way to get Dad over his obsession with that two centimetre lawn. Take him down to the garden centre to buy a water butt. This is a big container that collects rainwater. Bung one in your garden and pretty soon it will fill up – this is the UK after all! Rather than using water that's been purified with chemicals and come all the way from the river using energy to get here, use water that's fallen straight out of the sky. You can even get recycled water butts made from old tyres. If Dad leaves the lawn alone too, that means you're saving the world three times in one go!

No ifs and buts! A water butt saves precious rainwater
that's perfect for watering your garden.

Waste

Imagine if there was a room in your house where you put anything that you had finished with, or didn't want any more. Old baked bean tins, toys you played with when you were five, the cat litter, shampoo bottles, takeaway containers, that unfinished tin of paint. Imagine if you just made a huge pile of it and left it in the corner of your room. WHAT A SMELLY MESS! Well, believe it or not, that is what the INSANE adults do with your rubbish when you put it into the bin. Only instead of putting it in a corner of your room, the rubbish just goes into a big hole in a field, in the countryside.

These holes are called landfills and they're a complete eco-disaster. They're full of putrid old rubbish, like half-eaten hamburgers, old cigarette butts, filthy clothes, even 10-year-old nappies that wrapped your bottom when you were a baby! They're still stuck there, full of poo, whiling away the years and poisoning the ground below. You may think when the bin man comes and kindly wheels away your wheelie bin, that's the end of the matter. BUT THE RUBBISH REMAINS! It's still with us, in a landfill near you, creating a huge stink, destroying what was the home of animals everywhere.

The Mummyburger

Even things that would normally disappear in a few weeks in your compost, become mummified in landfill sites. In America, brave scientists with strong noses once dug into a landfill and found 10-year-old hamburgers, looking virtually like new. Yuk!

Where does uncycled rubbish go? Straight into a
big hole in the middle of the countryside.
What an ugly and destructive mess!

Reduce chemical spread

Put less in your bin! Many things made by humans now contain chemicals, which over time seep out and affect the soil around them. Bleach bottles or cans of hairspray contain toxic cocktails, which run through the soil. Eventually they find their way into water systems like lakes and rivers and poison fish. So, the less rubbish you end up putting into your bin, the better for the planet. Once again Super Kids, being a eco-hero involves the basics of life.

Buy biodegradable

Long word, brilliant meaning! Biodegradable stuff consists of things that can be made to disappear, by the natural forces on the planet. A brown paper bag, for example, is biodegradable. It can follow this perfect, natural cycle:

- ↺ When it rains, the bag gets wet.
- ↺ The wind pushes it against a rock face and breaks it up.
- ↺ The soil covers it, and bacteria and worms eat it.
- ↺ If the paper is chemical-free, it's returned to earth.
- ↺ Then the paper bag can become part of a tree again.

This is nature working miracles!

Avoid non-biodegradable

Many substances made by man are not biodegradable. Plastics, eco-heroes should be viewed with great suspicion. These are not biodegradable. When they escape into nature and get wet, they do not turn into mush. Instead, they resist the natural process of the weather and the soil, while plant roots cannot push through them and break them down.

Examples include your action man, a computer, a mobile phone – and don't forget the plastic boxes these all came in! Plastic containers from supermarkets or takeaways, the nets containing oranges or lemons, the chemical colourings that make the bright lettering on pizza boxes, cola cans, clothes made of synthetic fibres like nylon and polyester and old pairs of tights will all resist being broken down. Avoid them when you can!

Many of the things we use are not biodegradable.
After we throw them away, they'll still be here
for generations and generations.

Avoid packaged food

Ever noticed how many layers of plastic you have to battle through to get to your favourite snack? Nearly everything we buy these days comes pre-packaged and it creates huge amounts of waste. Some packaging is needed to keep certain foods like meat fresh – but the packaging may contain toxins! Next time you go shopping with Mum or Dad, note the amount of packaged food they buy – most of the trolley will be full of it. Suggest you shop at health food stores, or your local grocer and and butcher if you still have one. They use less packaging.

Farmers markets are also great places to buy food directly from the person who originally grew it. This food is very rarely pre-packaged. What's more, food from these places is mainly organic – ideal for Super Kids. See the Food section for more healthy food types.

Bad bag news

By feeding your Compost Monster (see the Garden section) one third of all the rubbish that would normally go in the bin, you reduce one third of the number of plastic bags you use, too. Plastic bags really are one of the planet's radical wrong-doers. If they escape the bin and then end up floating around the world, the mischief is immeasurable.

They get caught in the stomachs of cows, wrapped around the necks of turtles or seals, trapped on the feet of seagulls and float around on the seabed, never disappearing. Plastic bags should be at pole position in all Super Kids' eco-disaster files!

Try and avoid buying food that's covered in unnecessary
packaging. This means saving on plastic bags, too.

Reuse plastic bags

Just think, most plastic bags just get used once and then go into the bin when they would be used many times before their lives are over. While your Mum or Dad are stressing about getting ready to go to the supermarket, just grab a handful of plastic bags you have saved from last time. When you're at the checkout, get these out and pack the groceries in. Once again Super Kids, it may seem like a small and insignificant act – until you think of the one turtle you saved from a plastic death, one sea gull from plastic tummy-ache, one cow from plastic agony. You are an eco-hero!

Charity shops need our bags

To deal with the build-up of plastic bags, you can take them along to a charity shop to be reused. This is an ideal way of extending their useful lives. And helping others, too.

Almost everything can be recycled

Waste is so unnecessary in this day and age, when we can actually recycle the majority of non-biodegradable items.

Most councils have recycling schemes set up, where they provide special bins for each household to separate out their waste. Normally there are separate bins for paper, plastic and glass. These bins are collected and taken to recycling depots. Make sure your parents are recycling all they can and putting items in the right bins. If they say it's too much bother to separate everything, suggest they put recyclable items in a box, which you can sort out at the end of the week.

If your council does not have a recycling scheme, find out why not. Most councils have to reach recycling targets, so write them a letter demanding to know what's going on!

You may live in a rural area where there are too few people to set up a scheme. Then it's down to you to make a trip to your recycling depot or supermarket, which should have recycling bins. You could even form a neighbourhood group and take it in turns to take everyone's waste along.

Reuse them, recycle them, but whatever you do don't let your plastic bags get away. They can be killers!

Refill your bottle

As your mum reaches for those little bottles or paper cartons of fruit squash for your lunchbox, STOP HER! It's much better to buy concentrated fruit squash in a big bottle and refill a smaller one at home. You can reuse the same bottle every day.

Talking of squash

Stand in your kitchen, place your rubbish under your foot, and SQUASH! An eco-hero's work is never done. The less space your rubbish takes up, the smaller the landfill – or the more recycling you can fit in.

Plastic bottles

Plastic bottles are another major eco-enemy. In Britain, we use 15 million of them a day and only 3% are recycled. Here's a eco-hero fact for the Zombie Parents' dinner party – recycling one plastic bottle can save enough energy to power an electric light for six hours.

Make a sculpture from your rubbish

Tee hee hee, rubbish can be fun! Lots of the things we throw away can be made into art for school or home projects. You can make dragons from old cardboard, witches from wool and tin cans, snakes from sweet wrappers and mermaids from plastic bottles! Use your Super Kids' imagination. Be inspired to get creative by visiting www.childrensscrapstore.co.uk or www.bbc.co.uk/cbbc/bluepeter/.

SQUASH! FLATTEN! CRUSH! The smaller you can make your rubbish, the less room it will take up at the recycling plant or the rubbish tip.

Donate old magazines

You know how boring it can be, waiting to
see the doctor, especially when you feel like
you've got a monster up your nose! That's
when those magazines lying under your bed,
half-read, would be really useful. You'd also be
helping all the other miserable ill people enjoy some
distraction from their symptoms. So, do the world a
favour by donating all your old magazines to the doctor's
waiting room. Mum and Dad will be glad you've had a clear out, too.

Making paper is easy!

1. Soak some old newspapers in a bucket overnight, then drain off
the extra water. Using a liquidiser or wooden spoon, mash the paper
and water into a pulp. It should look a bit like wallpaper paste!
2. Put the pulp into a bowl with an equal volume of water and mix these
together. Then slide in some wire mesh and lift it out covered in pulp.
3. Place the mesh – pulp side down – quickly and carefully onto a clean,
flat cloth. Press down hard and peel off to leave the pulp on the cloth.
4. Put another cloth on top and press down firmly. Repeat these steps
with the remaining pulp then weight the pile down with something heavy.
5. After several hours gently peel away the paper. Leave pieces on some
kitchen towel, until completely dry. The paper is now ready to use!

Why not donate your old magazines and comics to your doctor's waiting room? A good way to reuse them and keep patients happy while they wait.

Food

You go down into the kitchen, open a packet of corn flakes, pour them into a bowl and start munching – but imagine if rather than being dumb, mindless cereal, your corn flakes could talk to you. What would they say? Their story goes something like this:

'I am a corn flake. Once I lived in a field. I grew on the top of a big green plant about as tall as your Mum. I had long luxurious leaves and all my friends grew around me. Twenty times during my short life of eight months or so, we were sprayed with some weird chemicals to kill off insects.'

'Then I was harvested and taken to the factory. There, I was cooked and pummelled into a paste. Salt, sugar and strange chemicals were added to make me stick together. Then I was squirted through a machine into little dollops and dried into my present unnatural shape. Making the box I live in cost the planet more energy than we give you, when you eat us.'

Food, Super Kids, is a big eco-dilemma. You gotta eat to stay alive. But one brand of biscuits or corn flakes may well have cost the planet a lot more than the next. You need to choose your belly fuel carefully.

Humans have been farming for 6,000 years, ever since we realised that growing plants was a better way to make sure we always had something to nosh on. But there are limits on how much food we can grow, including the soil getting worn out from being used so much, and insects competing to chomp on our grub.

In the 1950s humans invented 'brilliant new chemicals' to kill off insects and add nutrients to the soil for plants. Agriculture became 'intensive' – where only one type of crop was grown in a particular area – and more and more crops were planted on less space. These inventions have been really useful for feeding the 60 million people in Britain and the six billion people on the planet. But, the downside is their effects kill off all the insects and give a helping hand only to the plants we want. In lots of places, this has turned land into a kind of desert containing only one kind of plant, with very few insects or other wildlife.

Soil is made from old bits of dead animals and plants. It develops at a rate of a few millimetres a year. When humans expose it to the weather, through intensive agriculture, it can be lost at 100 times that rate. This is called soil erosion. More than 11% of the world's crop lands are severely eroded. Our land also becomes more salty when we water our crops. The resulting salination of soil is another big eco-problem.

These and other problems mean the brilliant green revolution solutions don't last long. Intensive agriculture means that eventually the amount of food we can grow, actually goes down. And then we really find ourselves in a pickle – more people, less food. In many parts of the world, farming has actually made the land into a real desert!

Become an organic farmer!

Growing organic is easier than it sounds. The perfect crop to try this out on is watercress. All you need is a packet of seeds from your local garden centre and a little plastic container with some soil. Plant your seeds and give them a good water. Then watch your harvest grow into a mini-crop of cress! OK, so it's not farming on a large scale, but it is organic. All it involves are the basic ingredients – seeds, soil, water, light and a little TLC from yourself. No pesticides or chemicals are needed or involved to boost growth.

This is how farming used to be done. Now farmers need to produce huge amounts with quick results. But there is an organic revolution going on. And it's the perfect fuel for Super Kids! Organic farms use a patchwork system with cows over here, sheep over there and perhaps some carrots and some corn. Most of the chemical pest killers are not allowed, so spiders and wildflowers – which also make great, free bug-assassins – can hang out safely.

SUPERFACT
500 chemicals are routinely used in normal farming, compared to four in organic farming.

Keep Mum sweet

It's not only fruit and veg that can carry the organic label – a far tastier example is chocolate. Your Mum's bound to enjoy organic food, even if she hasn't tried it yet. So why not treat her to a bar of organic chocolate for Mother's Day? Unlike normal chocolate bars, which contain sweeteners, organic chocolate contains far more of the stuff that actually makes it chocolate – cocoa powder. One tasty brand is Green and Black's. Buy her a bar and it's bound to convince her that organic is the way to go!

Try growing your own food organically. Once you get the bug, it might be hard to stop.

Fair deal

People slave away in warmer climates to grow the chocolate we gorge ourselves on, literally! People are paid so little and work in such poor conditions, it's barely better than slavery. Look out for the blue and green Fairtrade symbol. This means any profits made, go directly back to the cocoa bean growers, not the rich companies. See www.fairtrade.org.uk.

FAIRTRADE
Guarantees
a **better deal**
for Third World
Producers

SUPERFACT
99% of the world's coffee is not fairly traded. So millions of growers receive less than 1% of the price we pay in coffee bars and shops.

Is your school Fairtrade friendly?

Does your school support Fairtrade food? Ask your teachers and canteen staff. If they don't, ask why not and recommend that they do! Another alternative is to hold Fairtrade days, when you can set up stalls at lunch-time to sell Fairtrade products.

SUPERFACT
One quarter of all Central American rainforest has already been cut down to make cattle ranches. Most of the beef goes to the hamburger trade in North America.

Be burger aware

Eating a beefburger may be helping to destroy the rainforest! Most burgers in Britain are made from European cattle, but these cattle are often fed on soya beans. A lot of this comes from Brazil, where large areas of the rainforest have been destroyed to make soya fields. Before buying a burger, first ask where the cattle came from and what they were fed on.

Before buying a burger, ask where the cattle came from and what they were fed on.

Buy produce when it's in season

Know your seasons, Super Kids. Different types of food grow at different times of the year. Somehow we've got used to having any old fruit and veg whenever we want, flown in from other countries where the weather is different. The fuel that flies this produce round the world adds to global warming too! You can really save the world – and have something to look forward to – by eating seasonal food that's grown in the UK, as below:

FOOD CALENDAR

JANUARY
Cabbage, cauliflower, celeriac, leeks, parsnips, turnip, shallots, squash

FEBRUARY
Cabbage, cauliflower, celeriac, chard, chicory, kohlrabi, leeks, parsnips, spinach, swede, turnip

MARCH
Beetroot, cabbage, cauliflower, leeks, mint, parsley, broccoli, radishes, rhubarb, sorrel

APRIL
Broccoli, cabbage, cauliflower, radishes, rhubarb, carrots, kale, watercress, spinach

MAY
Broccoli, cabbage, cauliflower, gooseberries, parsley, mint, broad beans, rhubarb, new carrots, asparagus

JUNE
Carrots, cherries, lettuce, strawberries, peppers, peas, rhubarb, gooseberries, tomatoes, broad beans, asparagus

JULY
Carrots, gooseberries, strawberries, spinach, tomatoes, watercress, loganberries, cauliflower, aubergine, fennel, asparagus, cabbage, celery, cherries, lettuce, mangetout, new potatoes, peas, radishes, raspberries, rhubarb, tomatoes, French beans

AUGUST
Carrots, gooseberries, lettuce, loganberries, raspberries, strawberries, cauliflower, aubergines, nectarines, peaches, peppers, courgettes, rhubarb, sweetcorn, greengages, basil, peas, pears, apples, French beans, tomatoes

SEPTEMBER
Apples, aubergines, blackberries, cabbage, carrots, cauliflower, cucumber, damsons, figs, French beans, grapes, lettuce, melons, onions, mushrooms, peppers, peas, parsnips, pears, potatoes, pumpkin, raspberries, rhubarb, spinach, sweetcorn, tomatoes

OCTOBER
apples, aubergines, cabbage, carrots, cauliflower, lettuce, marrow, mushrooms, parsnips, potatoes, tomatoes

NOVEMBER
cabbage, pumpkin, swede, cauliflower, potatoes, parsnips, pears, leeks, quinces, chestnuts, cranberries, beetroot

DECEMBER
Celery, cabbage, red cabbage, cauliflower, celeriac, pumpkin, beetroot, turnips, parsnips, sprouts, pears, swede

Know your seasons and know your vegetables, and you'll be able to enjoy good local food all year round.

Take a map to the supermarket

Make a rough world guide for your trolley and use it to work out how far the food there has travelled. You might find blueberries from Egypt, broccoli from Bulgaria and bananas from Bahamas. Between them they've come thousands of miles! OK, bananas don't think much of our wet weather, so they need to travel if we are to have them at all. The best way to help is to know your geography and try to buy things from the closest country – or better still, home – to reduce your air miles.

Good Milk

Did you know that some dairy cows actually have their calves taken from them, the very day they are born? Sometimes the cows call for their lost young for weeks afterwards. Most milk is produced this way, but some organic milk farmers allow the young ones to stay with their mums for much longer. They keep them in a pen next to mum, so they can see and talk to each other. Organic milk from organic cows is not only better for you, with extra vitamins and antioxidants – it's better for the cows, too!

Keep your own chickens

The most useful pet is a chicken, especially if you love eggs. Chickens need a coop to live in, a safe place to run around in your garden and some grain to eat. You can even re-home battery chickens after their life in the battery unit. Battery chickens are only kept for as long as they produce at least one egg a day. Sadly, they tend to be killed when they are 18 months old. You can keep them at home well past this age and they will still make a lot of eggs for you.

BLACKMOOR FARM ←

There's no doubt about it, locally grown food is best.
It's a good idea to pay for it though!

Fishy facts

Once upon a time, people fished in small boats with a rod and line or with nets. They caught enough to feed their family and maybe sell on a few fish to make some money. The fish did fine – they lost a few friends, but that's all. Now Super Kids, fisheries are mega, mega business. Huge fishing vessels drop nets which are 80 miles long, to catch 85 million tons of fishy harvest a year. Between 1950 and today, the amount of fish dragged out of the sea has increased four times over. There used to be 17 big fisheries. These are places around the oceans of the world, where fish congregate and people catch them. In recent years four of them have disappeared and nine are on their way out. Why? Because some of the fish worth catching are gone.

Eating fish is really good for us – roughly one in every five mouthfuls of protein we eat comes from fish – but we're running out of them. How do we balance this up?

Buy sustainably harvested fish

Sustainable fishing is when fishermen catch some fish, but leave enough to keep breeding. They can do this by having nets that allow little fish to escape, grow full size and have young. Next time Mum or Dad

say fish is on the menu, ask whether it's sustainable. If not, tell them to look for the logo of the Marine Stewardship Council. This identifies the best environmental choice in seafood. You can find out where to buy MSC labelled products at www.msc.org.

SUPERFACT

More than one in four of all fish caught are thrown back dead. That's 27 million tons every year!

Cut it out

The other way of not depleting the world's fish stocks, is to avoid eating them altogether. If that's your choice, you need to make sure you replace the health-giving oils in fish with other sources of 'good fat'. These can be found in many vegetables and plant extracts, including nuts, seeds and beans. A handful a day is all you need!

If left unchecked, the fishing industry could steadily
destroy all the world's fish stocks.

Use your Super Kids' detective skills!

Be wary of children's menus at restaurants. They often offer cheap, processed foods, packed full of additives and unhealthy ingredients. Be careful of products selling themselves as 'low-sugar' or 'sugar-free'. They probably contain artificial sweeteners, which are nasty man-made ingredients.

Wash and peel

Feeling hungry? Apples are the perfect quick, healthy snacks for Super Kids. But before you bite into that Granny Smith or Cox's, wait a minute. Have you washed it? Some apples have been sprayed 16 times with 36 different chemicals, according to a 1998 government report. So always make sure you wash, and if necessary peel, any fresh fruit and vegetables to get rid of all those horrible pesticides.

SUPERFACT
20% of the Earth's land surface is too dry for agriculture. About 20% is too cold, 20% is too mountainous and 20% is forested or too marshy. That leaves only 20% suitable for growing food.

Choose one organic product to buy regularly

The more people demand organic food products, the more farmers will decide to produce them – and the cheaper they will become. Convince Mum or Dad to buy one organic product, like milk, bread or eggs, regularly. It's a good way of getting them into the organic shopping routine.

Get cooking!

Next time you go to a birthday party, why not take some organic biscuits or cakes you've made yourself? If you learn to cook just one dish a month, in a year's time you'll have 12 different dishes you can share with friends and family. If you're looking for inspiration, **www.organics.org** has loads of cool recipes and cooking advice.

Next time you go to a birthday party, how about taking some biscuits you've made. Much more fun than a present – and tastier too.

RED ALERT! FRANKENSTEIN'S MONSTER IS LOOSE!

The adults are really getting themselves into trouble now. They've started messing around with the very basis of life – DNA!

DNA is this brilliant stuff inside us, which tells our growing body what to be like. If you've got brown eyes, then somewhere inside you is a bit of DNA telling your body to make the brown pigment to give your that eye colour. If your hair is wild and curly or straight and fine, then inside the cells of your body is a little code for that too. Inside every single cell of our bodies there is a list of instructions for making YOU.

And inside your friend's body there is a different list, telling their body how to make them. We are all unique because of this special code. A lettuce has its own code, as does a tomato and a cat!

Now, mad humans have started to mess around with this very essence of life. They have started making weird creatures, using random bits of DNA, all stitched together.

SUPERFACT
To find out where to buy locally produced food that hasn't been flown halfway round the world, or contains GM ingredients, visit www.bigbarn.co.uk.

It's just not sensible, eco-warriors. We don't know what we're doing! Once again, humans are meddling in the beautiful order of things. Something that has taken billions of years to get right. Believe it Super Kids, scientists are taking genes from one animal – like a salmon – and putting them into another, like a sheep. It's scary stuff!

And they're doing it with plants, too. They call them 'genetically modified' or GM, because their genes have been changed. Refuse these foods. Only buy foods that are labelled to say they don't contain GM ingredients.

Just how far will scientists go as they mix and match
the genes of different animals?

Be selective

If your Zombie Mum or Dad prefers shopping at big supermarkets to local food stores, make sure the food they buy bears a 'British' stamp of approval. Or look out for the Little Red Tractor stamp. This covers all standards of production on the farm, from levels of wildlife, to food hygiene, safety and how animals are cared for.

Who makes your favourite food?

Find out more about the big names behind your favourite sweets and chocolate. These big companies wield a lot of power, but it's down to us to make sure they spend their money wisely. If you hear something bad about a company, do some research and decide for yourself whether you think there's some truth in it. If enough people stop buying their products, this sends out a big message to these companies.

Cut back on meat

You really only need to eat meat about two or three times a week. Bacon for breakfast, steak for lunch and sausages for tea really is much too much, even for a Super Kid saving the world! Try a few tasty vegetarian meals instead. Even if you're not a veggie it's a good way to get your greens. Check out the Vegetarian Society website at **www.vegsoc.org** for ideas.

Think of the animals

Farmers in this country have found life very hard recently. The last thing we want to do is make life any harder for them. But the animals need a break too. The Food Animal Initiative, based at Oxford University, is finding out how to make the lives of farm animals easier, without making things any harder for the farmers. Find out more at **www.faifarms.co.uk**.

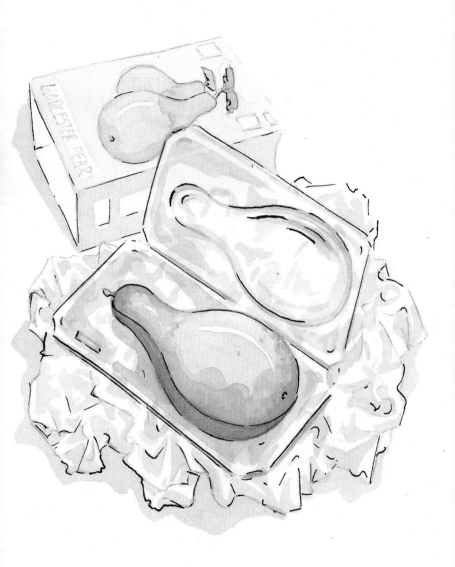

**Try not to buy food that comes in too much packaging.
Does that fruit really need to be individually wrapped?**

Home and School

Scientists have shown over and over again, that the older you get, the more stuck your brain becomes. Like your body, your brain slows down and even goes into reverse as the ageing process takes hold. Habits that started when you were very young, stay with you as you grow, and it becomes harder to do anything new.

Your poor Zombie Parents are probably stuck. They have grown up unaware of their impact on the world. They march through life, tired and overstretched, sitting in traffic jams, staring at computers, watching the washing machine go round and round. They are too obsessed with the whiteness of your t-shirts or the shininess of their car to save the world.

But Zombie Adults don't need telling off, or scorning. They desperately need our help. They need explaining the right way to go about things. And they need information that can help lift them out of Zombiness and back into humanity.

And that, Super Kids, is where you come in – at home and at school.

Zombie adults don't need telling off. They desperately need our help to learn about their impact on the world.

Write right

Is your mum always leaving lists and notes around the house to remind her to do things? Half the time these lists get lost and forgotten about. And then she blames you for not reminding her to collect the stuff from the dry-cleaners! Why not suggest getting a house whiteboard you can put up where everyone will see it. This is the perfect way to leave any messages and reminders for each other because it doesn't waste paper.

Start a paper round

Zombie Parents get through a lot of newspaper reading! But where does all that paper go? If your council doesn't have a recycling box scheme, then try your local supermarket. Recommend a weekly household recycling day to coincide with when your Mum or Dad goes shopping.

POOPERFACTS!
● Disposable nappies form about 4% of all household waste in the UK.
● Each baby will use an average of 6,500 disposable nappies from birth to potty training. Compare that to 50 cotton ones!
● Decomposing disposable nappies emit noxious methane gas. It takes 200 – 500 years for a disposable nappy to decompose.

Eco-baby

Do you have a baby brother or sister who needs greening? Is he or she walking around in a nappy, which takes a cup of crude oil to make? Plastic disposable nappies are a nightmare, eco-kids. They use up fossil fuels to make, then lie around in a landfill for centuries. Get that little sprog into greener nappies. Use cloth nappies and a nappy washing service. Or bung their bums inside compostable nappies. Visit **www.wen.org.uk** to find out more.

Blackboards and whiteboards are great ways to get messages across – without wasting any paper.

RED ALERT: CHEMICAL NIGHTMARE

More than 400 toxic chemicals have been discovered INSIDE the human body. Your body just doesn't understand or know what to do with these chemicals. There are also around 60,000 chemicals in daily use! It's a massive experiment with the human body. We haven't got a clue what we're doing, and we don't really know what the chemicals might do to us either. We just pour them on our hair as shampoo, eat them in weirdly coloured sweets, spray them all over our houses, gardens, cars, clothes, shoes and each other. And yet, we know the number of people suffering with cancer increased by 77% between 1982 and 1992. What we don't know is why — but it could be because of these chemicals. So stay on the safe side. Always read the label and reduce the chemical burden in your home.

> **SUPERFACT**
> One in eight children has asthma in the UK. This figure has increased six-fold in the last 25 years.

Can't breathe?

You walk into the living room and there's your Zombie Mum, about to spray furniture polish onto the sideboard. STOP HER! She might be making the inside of your house smell like roses, or a summer's day, but by assaulting your lungs with unnecessary chemicals, she could also be putting you more at risk of suffering from asthma. Remind your Mum how important breathing is, and that it could affect her too.

Learn how to green clean

● Get clothes sparkling with one cup of finely grated soap, one cup of washing soap and two tablespoons of lavender oil.

● Use white chalk to get any mucky stains off your clothes — just rub it on before they go in the wash.

● Forget bleach. Bicarbonate of soda is great for cleaning sinks and baths.

● A little bit of vinegar on newspaper is the best way to dissolve oily marks on windows.

● Try olive oil and vinegar to polish furniture, too.

**Show your Mum how destructive cleaning chemicals
can be, when released into the air you breathe.
Remind her she's breathing them in too!**

Pick it up!

Just because it's on the floor, doesn't mean it's dirty. Ask yourself, does that jumper or those jeans really need a wash? You could reduce your washing load by as much as half by folding up, putting away and wearing clothes, which aren't really dirty. The less you wash your clothes, the less water, energy and chemicals you'll use. And by tidying up your room in the process, you'll be giving your Zombie Mum or Dad a break too!

Have sweet dreams

Your Zombie Parents have finally given in and allowed you to decorate your bedroom. It's time for some creativity, Super Kids! What about having some cool animal stencils or a jungle theme? But wait! Before you get carried away, check to make sure your new room is being given the eco-friendly treatment. Go with your Zombie Parents to get the paint – you'll need to anyway, to make sure they don't just buy boring magnolia! Check that the paint you buy is natural and mineral-based. Chances are the rest of your house has been painted with solvent-based or gloss paint. These are bad for humans and the environment, too. They contain nasty ingredients called Volatile Organic Compounds (VOCs). If inhaled or absorbed through the skin, they can irritate your eyes, nose and throat. They can even affect your internal organs. To help you and your Zombie Parents find natural paints visit **www.ecosolutions.co.uk** or **www.auroorganic.co.uk.**

Lighten up

Did you know energy-saving light bulbs last eight times as long as normal light bulbs? Which means not only do they help save the planet, they save you money too. It's a good way to persuade your Zombie Parents to change all the bulbs in your house!

Next time you're redecorating your room, try to use natural paint that doesn't contain toxins. Fruit juice is even more natural – but that might be going a bit far!

Help the Homeless

While you're cosily tucked up on the sofa watching TV, between 310,00 and 380,000 homeless people are out on the streets, hoping they'll survive the cold for another night. You can support

them by buying *The Big Issue*. The people who sell it on the streets are registered homeless and sell the magazine to make some money for food and shelter. It's packed with interesting stories and facts too!

Join the tribal quest

While we may be happy in our homes, taking four walls and a roof for granted, lots of people are having theirs chopped down around their ears! There are about 1,000 tribes who live in the rainforests of the world. These indigenous tribes (this means they come from the area they now live in) have been there for thousands of years. In some parts of South East Asia and the Pacific Islands, they have been there for about 40,000 years!

These tribes have managed to develop ways of life, which allow them to use the forest without destroying it. While other civilisations have grown further and further away from the natural world, rainforest tribes have had to grow closer to nature, in order to survive. They understand the environment in which they live, better than we understand our own. The trouble is, they're running out of forest to live in.

Many native tribes are now extinct because of interference from the western world. Find out how you can help these amazing people at www.survival-International.org.

SUPERFACT

For every homeless person in England, there are at least two empty homes, and 10% of them belong to local authorities. The Empty Houses Agency campaigns to raise awareness of this problem and promotes solutions to bring empty houses into use again.

Would you like it if someone came round and chopped
down your home? That's what's happening to the people
who live in the world's rainforests.

School daze

They say education is all about the three 'Rs' – Reading, wRiting and aRithmetic, but now it's time to add three more; Reduce, Reuse and Recycle!

There's tons of stuff you can do in school to cut back on the amount of paper used. If your school is eco-friendly, they should be doing this already. Have a look at the list below, to see whether your school is doing enough. Don't be afraid to suggest new ideas to your teachers. It will show that you're taking responsibility to help solve issues facing society – in true Super Kids style!

✔ Make sure your school is buying paper, pencils and other products made from recycled materials. If not, help teachers source some at www.recycledproducts.org.uk.

✔ Just like at home, set up a system for collecting used paper from classrooms and offices. Then take it to the main recycling bin at the end of every day or week. Your local authority recycling officer can give you some advice and maybe even some proper collection bins.

✔ Use both sides of the paper for writing, drawing or photocopying. Set up a collection tray in each classroom, for paper that's only been used on one side.

✔ Reuse old card, coloured paper and glossy magazines in artwork. And turn old paper into models using papier-maché.

✔ Bring old copies of the Yellow Pages to school for recycling – you can get environmental educational materials in return! Find out more at www.yellow-woods.co.uk.

✔ Reuse old envelopes by sticking a label over the previous address. You can send an email to ask for envelope reuse stickers to Julie@wastewatch.org.uk.

✔ Email newsletters about your eco-activities to parents. Or post information on your school website. Spread the word the eco-way!

Try recycling your old yellow pages directories – it can be monstrously good fun.

It's a jungle out there

Why not turn the school playground into a area for lots of creatures, plants and flowers — not just kids? Can you plant some trees, allow a bit of grass to grow wild or build a little pond? There are more than 30,000 schools in the UK, and an eco-area in every school ground would make a huge difference to our levels of wildlife.

Get some cash!

Once the site of the wildlife area has been decided on, the next stage is to get some money from funders to put your ideas into action. It may be possible to get a pile of money or grant from your local council. A county council, city council or the London Borough, should have a number of officers responsible for local environmental management. The conservation officer will probably be very happy to help out with advice, and hopefully financial assistance! Find out from your Town Hall, if your local authority has an environmental co-ordinator. This is a person you can contact, who makes sure that the planet gets some help and attention.

Raise funds, raise awareness, raise some laughs

Why not tell your school friends about the amazing things you've learned from this book. You could organise an eco-group at school. All you need is a place and time to meet, and some posters telling people all about it. Maybe a not-so-Zombie Teacher could help?

You could just be a talking group, with one person each week giving a little speech on what they've discovered. Or you could organise more eco-activities like recycling, getting kids to turn off lights or buy fewer fizzy drinks. Or try a rag day where kids pay £1 to wear their own clothes instead of uniform. You could use the money to help fund your wildlife area. Find out more at www.eco-schools.org.uk. Or sign up your school to Action at School with Global Action Plan at **www.globalactionplan.org.uk.**

Try turning your school playground into a living jungle.

Pets

Your number one assistant in your mission to save the planet may be your dog, cat or hamster, but they've got to be Super Pets. It's no good protecting the world, if you're not already protecting your pet. It's also no good protecting the world, if your pet is destroying it right behind you!

Animals, like sheep, pigs and cows, have been living with us for a long time. We use these animals for their meat, milk, and wool, but there are some that live alongside us and are treated like members of the family. They're our pets, and the only thing we want from them is their love and company.

We have to be careful which pets we choose. Not all creatures are as comfortable with human company as cats and dogs. Imagine if a parrot took you from your home, squeezed you into a box with hundreds of other kids, then put you in a cage and forced you to eat food you didn't like. Not a nice thought! Yet that's what we humans do to so many of the pets that make their way into our homes.

Meanwhile, there's a potential eco-threat from a surprising source. It might even be curled up on the sofa by your side. Your little puddy cat may seem loving enough when she's tilting her head asking for an ear scratch. But when she exits the cat-flap, an altogether different animal takes over. Cats can still be predators and massacre 200 million small birds and mammals a year in Britain — if you let them.

So much to consider, Super Kids, so much to do! Time to turn the page.

In countries like New Zealand, where flightless birds
once waddled round with no fear of predators, the
introduction of pet cats has helped drive some of
them to the edge of extinction.

Green your pooch

Who would have thought old Rover could be a danger! He may be your best friend, but if a little kid comes into contact with your dog's poo in the park, it can be a serious health hazard.

Dog poo contains worms, which in true Alien style can burrow inside the human body and make a life for themselves there. It's a truly nasty business!

SUPERFACT
Lobbying by conservation organisations and the public means 100 airlines now refuse to carry parrots caught in the wild.

So, Super Kids, BAG AND BIN! Always carry newspaper with you when you're walking your dog. If he feels the need to drop a number two in a public place, simply pick up the poo in the paper and put in the poo-bin. Never use plastic bags, as the poo will just sit inside forever. If your local park doesn't have a poo-bin, write to the local council insisting they get one.

Vet your pets

Know anyone who owns an iguana or a snake in their living room? Got a friend who fancies cuddling up to a koala bear or hiding a terrapin in their bath tub? It's time to have a word with them. Remind them that many unusual animals brought into this country have been snatched from the wild and squashed into cages for a long sea journey. If they don't die, they end up in an environment that doesn't suit them. In fact, the pet trade has a lot to answer for. Tortoises, for example, have become so rare it's now illegal to own them if they've come from the wild. Luckily, conservation efforts are now being made in the Mediterranean countries where they live, to stop them disappearing forever. For more helpful advice about pets visit www.vet2pet.co.uk.

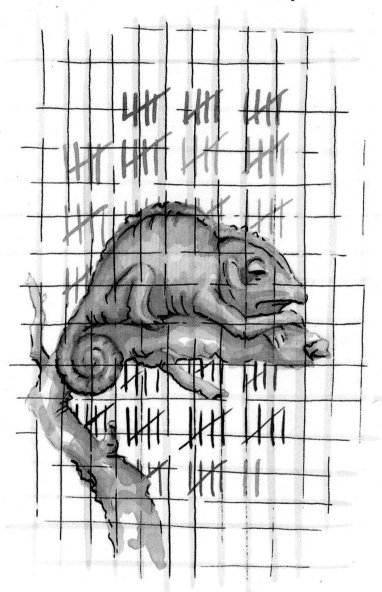

For many animals brought into this country, their
caged life can be like a jail sentence.
And no one wants a grumpy pet.

Support the RSPCA

The RSPCA looks after animals who have been abandoned or neglected by their owners – or whose owners can't care for them anymore. If you want to buy a pet, why not start by visiting their website at **www.rspca.org.uk**.

SUPERFACT

Every year the RSPCA receives 1.5 million calls for assistance. They investigate over 120,000 complaints about cruelty to animals in England and Wales, and convict more than 3,000 people of being cruel.

WORLD GONE MAD WARNING!
NOT OK CORAL!

Coral reefs are almost as rich in wildlife as tropical forests. They are dream-like places where intricate, colourful and beautiful fish swim among the rocks and anemones. But these fish need to stay where they are. Believe it or not, some mad adults actually BOMB coral reefs, collect the fish that survive there and transport them hundreds of miles around the world to be put into aquariums – just like in Finding Nemo. If you ever see an aquarium in someone's house, at the doctor's or in a restaurant, ask the owner if they know where the fish came from. And if they don't, MAKE THEM SQUIRM!

Naughty kitty!

Even well-fed pet cats kill birds and mammals in your garden, so take decisive action. Attach two bells firmly to your cat's collar and she won't be able to surprise her prey! It's important to use two bells because clever cats can work out how to silence one bell, but not both.

If your cat is a killer, attach two bells to its collar to give birds and small mammals a chance to get away.

Be dog friendly

Did you know that greyhounds were bred to run at 40 miles an hour to hunt hares, deer and rabbits? Or that terriers were designed to dive into holes to grab foxes, rabbits and rats?

All dogs have been bred by humans for a particular job. Many of them find it really difficult to adjust when we own them as pets, and don't let them do the job their brain is telling them to do. Many pets even end up homeless because their owners can't put up with their antics.

The key, Super Kids, is NEVER JUDGE A DOG BY ITS COVER! Always research the breed's behaviour before you buy to be sure that's what you really want.

SUPERFACT

Did you know, around 30% of Britain's pets are overweight? Most pet-owners are guilty of feeding their pet too many snacks. This can be just as cruel as underfeeding. Porky pets suffer discomfort, have shorter lives, and recover from surgery or disease less well.

Be space savvy

Too many of the cages we keep our pets in are little more than prison cells. Animals need room to get about, jump around and take some well-needed exercise in. That can add up to a lot of space. And humans cannot always supply anywhere near the kind of room or freedom some animals need to stay happy and healthy.

So plan ahead, Super Kids! Check with the RSPCA to find out exactly what requirements each pet will need. Then measure out the space you've got available at home. If it's not enough, it's time to look for something else.

Examine the space you've got available for your pet very carefully – small homes and cages make unhappy pets.

Outside your back door, a jungle is lurking. Your back yard or garden could be home to the most exotic creatures – in their own small way as ferocious as a tiger or as exciting as a dolphin. The trouble is that modern gardens are often animal assault courses, full of chemicals to slay the little creatures, lawnmowers to massacre them, cats to kill them and no food to feed them. You can change all that, Super Kids.

Zombie Parents tend to be one of two kinds, when it comes to their gardens. They either do nothing, or they're obsessed with tidying. If yours are in the first category, leave them alone and get on with creating your own mini-wilderness in the wreckage they've left.

If they're the tidying type though, you're in trouble. And so are the creatures depending on your plot for a living! Mowing the grass till it resembles a grade-two skinhead is a huge waste-of-time – second only to Mum's obsession with polishing furniture or whitening your clothes. Life is meant to be fun and bursting with energy, not always neat and orderly.

In fact, there's a great word to learn, that explains all this. That word is ENTROPY. This is the tendency of all things towards MAXIMUM DISORDER. In other words, no matter how much you wash up or mow the lawn, you will never finish. That's because systems – like the car, the lawn or even the universe – have a tendency to be chaotic.

So, the next time your Mum or Dad start talking about tidying up the garden, quote the law of entropy to them. Then get out into the garden and start reinstating that wilderness.

Entropy is the tendency of all things towards maximum disorder. And that goes for mowing the lawn, too.

Avoid nasty chemicals

If the company that makes the chemicals that people use on their rose gardens, can't persuade your Zombie Parents to buy them, they won't make any money. So, they tell your parents they NEED them, to kill off any insects who live there. The trouble is, when you kill the insects, you kill the birds and the hedgehogs. Foxes, squirrels and mice are affected along the food chain, too. Don't let them spray chemicals. Tell them you like the insects – and so do the birds.

Slugs and snails

Are cute really! And they fill up the bellies of frogs and thrushes. There's ways to combat them without putting down nasty chemicals, which make them die a horrible death:

✔ Buy naturally slug-resistant plants, like cornflowers, marigolds, geraniums, and sweet peas.

✔ Spread ash, beer or eggshell around your favourite plants to protect them from unwanted visitors. Or plant lavender or rosemary nearby – slugs hate the smell.

✔ Get to know your snails, by dabbing non-toxic paint on their backs. You can even number them and follow them in their escapades round your garden.

Make a pile of rocks

And the frogs will shelter underneath. Being amphibians, they need to keep their skin damp all the time. They love to snooze in the dark, dankness under stones and inside old flower pots.

Number the shells of snails you find with non-toxic paint.
You'll be able to identify them again later.

Build a pond!

Making a pond is a great task for your Zombie Mum or Dad to help you with. When you've dug out your hole, you'll need some kind of liner like rubber or clay to keep the water in. Now it's time to imagine yourself as a frog or bird, trying to get into the pond. It needs to slope gently downwards, so you can waddle in or drink some water. Don't forget you need to be able to get back out again! Remember that water is the most precious thing on earth, so everyone will benefit, from toadlets to hedgehogs.

Stock your pond with oxygen-giving plants like water lilies. Underwater plants like water milfoil and water starwort are great too. Find them all at your local garden centre or pet shop. Best leave out the goldfish, though — they eat the eggs of wild animals like frogs, toads and newts.

In the summer, evaporation from the heat will cause the water level of your pond to drop. So remember to keep your pond topped up.

Remove leaves in autumn. When they rot this can make the pond stagnant. Use them as compost instead.

SUPERFACT
Scientists who raised the temperature of ponds by 3°C, to mimic the effect of global warming, found it wiped out fish, small animals and plants.

Stop mowing the grass

How can anything live in a centimetre high patch of grass? It's time to stop your Mum or Dad mowing down those blades of grass. Make them put their feet up. Or get them to help you make that pond.

Your parents will love what you do with your pond.
But you'd better warn them of your plans first!

Be a friend to frogs

If you want to feed hedgehogs, give them tinned cat or dog food (not fish-based), scrambled eggs, chicken leftovers, chopped peanuts, grated cheese or breakfast cereal. But don't ever give them milk — they can't digest it.

Turn your bonfire before you light it

Do you known what's inside the lovely pile of leaves, logs and old bits of furniture that makes up your bonfire? There could be a hedgehog, who thinks she's found a deluxe residence. She doesn't know she's about to be scorched. If she crawled in some weeks ago, she may be hibernating and too sleepy to crawl out in time!

Save her, Super Kids. Turn your bonfire over before you set fire to it, to check there's no one living inside. To help any slow creatures like beetles and woodlice escape, light the fire from one side so they can crawl out of the other.

Pet worms

Here's a wriggly little idea. You can now buy special kits to collect your worms in. Why bother? Because it's fun. And because worms make amazing compost to use on your plants.

A worm can recycle half its own body weight of kitchen waste every day! Tiger worms or red worms are the best types to use. You can even BUY WORMS! Contact Wiggly Wigglers for more details at www.wigglywigglers.co.uk.

Turn over your bonfire before you set light to it – you
never know what might be hiding underneath.

Love your dead wood

The first thing most gardeners will do with a fallen branch is put it on the fire or in the bin. Stop them! Don't they know that without the thousands of wildlife like fungi and beetles, which live in dead wood, everyone starves? Don't they realise they will be killing generations of creatures, by casually throwing away their only source of food?

Leave the dead wood in your garden. Fungal spores grow microscopic roots, which push their way through the body of the dead wood and break it up, so beetles and other insects, like woodlice and termites, can munch. Then down comes a nuthatch or a blue tit to eat the insect larvae or feed them to their chicks. This is called a food chain.

There's a whole web of life starting in that one old branch. If your Mum or Dad don't like the look of old wood, hide your branch in a special place behind the shed or compost heap. Just don't let them throw it away – it's a living banquet for non-human folk!

Plant a fruit tree or an orchard

The most exciting things to grow, are those you can eat afterwards. And fruit trees will supply you with tasty, juicy goodness for years to come.

It's not just you and your family that will enjoy the fruit, though. It's also a tasty treat for birds, voles, mice, insects and even butterflies that love to drink the sweet juice of an apple or pear.

You might even end up with squiffy blue tits, spiders or squirrels in your garden – animals have been known to get drunk after eating the flesh of fermenting fruit!

Don't let that old dead tree get cut down.
It's a banquet for wildlife.

Feed the birds

The best time of year to feed birds is in the winter, when their natural source of food is scarce. Once you've started putting out food though, you have to do it everyday – especially in winter. Stop suddenly, and there won't be enough food for all the birds you've attracted to the area.

Gardens have become places where countryside birds, finding intensive agriculture a bit unfriendly, like to visit. You can make your garden really homely, friendly and welcoming, by feeding the birds.

You can buy special seed, or feed them wholemeal bread, bits of fruit, coconut, cooked rice, pastry, and fat like bacon rind or lard. They even like cooked pasta!

Why not try out the delicious recipe opposite – delicious for birds that is!

Make a bird cake

First make a mould – half a coconut shell with string or wire threaded through a hole in the base makes a good one. An empty yoghurt pot works well too.

Ingredients:

- **500g fat** (suet is best)
- **500g mixed bird seed**
- **750g scraps** (biscuit or cake crumbs, grated cheese, minced peanuts, sultanas and brown bread are good)

Method:

1. Carefully melt fat in a large saucepan – don't make it too hot. Stir in all the other ingredients.

2. Pour into mould and leave to set. Yoghurt pot cakes need wire pushed into the middle, while soft.

3. Hang coconut moulds as they are, upside down in the garden. Yoghurt pot cakes need to be pressed out first.

SUPERFACT

Can you spot the UK's five commonest garden birds? According to Garden Birdwatch, they are:

1. House sparrow   2. Starling   3. Blue tit
4. Blackbird   5. Greenfinch

Your bird cake shapes are limited only by your imagination. It's all about the moulds you use!

Give an owl a home

You can encourage the most amazing creatures to live close to your home, right in your own garden, if you offer them a nest box – and there aren't many creatures more amazing than owls.

Owls love to live in old trees or buildings, but lots of old trees are now removed by Zombie Adults obsessed with tidying. Or old buildings are made into new houses for humans. Owls will happily live inside a special wooden owl box, which you can attach to your home, shed or garden tree. You might even end up with young owlets in your garden! See the Hawk and Owl Trust for more information at **www.hawkandowl.org**.

SUPERFACT
A bee's wings beat an amazing 11,400 times a minute. And a bumblebee can carry 60% of its own body weight in pollen!

Be kind to bees

There are around 25,000 different species of bee in the world. Bees and other insects do a marvellous job, carrying pollen from flower to flower. They need bees to help them reproduce. Without this pollination service, flowers would not be able to live. And remember, one-third of the food we eat is pollinated by them.

But something is afoot eco-kids. All over the world, bee numbers have been massively reduced by chemicals, disease or habitats being destroyed. Help them recover by giving bees a nest. Plant their favourite food in your garden, and when one lands on you, don't brush her away – she's unlikely to sting unless you make her. For more information on looking after bees in your garden, visit the Oxford Bee Company at **www.oxbeeco.com**.

this Property
reserved for
A. Nowl

Do what you can to encourage owls to live in your
garden. Just remember one thing, though – owls
may be wise, but they can't read!

Make friends with the Compost Monster

Before you leave for school, you have to feed the Monster at the bottom of your garden. What do you mean you don't have one? Make one today! The Compost Monster (Zombie Parents probably just call it a compost heap), is a magnificent pile of any old rubbish that used to be alive. Got some old fruit, vegetable ends, paper (made from trees) or grass cuttings? Just chuck it on the Monster and he'll turn it into something new! That's because he's made up of the bacteria and moulds that grow on all that old rubbish, and the worms and beetles that love to munch on it. The result? You can spread the compost made from all this organic churning onto your garden. This is how to fertilise your plants, the natural way.

Give him a home

The Compost Monster needs something to contain him — or he has a habit of spreading about all over the place! You can put him in a ready-made plastic bin. Then just lift the lid to say hello or when you need to feed him. Or you can make him a special wooden crate, a bit like a dog house.

SUPERFACT

Cosy compost loves a warm environment. The more heat in your compost heap, the more quickly you can use it. The peak temperature for compost is a steamy 60°C!

Remember to feed him everyday

It's amazing what the Compost Monster likes to be fed. Tea bags, tea leaves, toilet paper (it was once wood!) egg shells or grass cuttings — these can all be part of the daily intake he needs. And just think, everything you pour into his great big mouth gets put to good use — not poured into landfill sites across the country. Find out more about compost at www.hdra.org.uk.

FEED ME! FEED ME NOW!
When your Compost Monster calls, you
better come running!

Go batty

Bats are less 'evil vampires' and more 'amazing creatures'. They are just brilliant at what they do — detecting the tiniest of insects, while flying at 30 miles an hour through the air. IN THE PITCH DARK! This, Super Kids, is a real super-power.

Tragically, all the species of bat in Britain are in decline. Why? Because their homes and the insects they feed on are getting harder to come by. Bats need roosts to sleep in, maternity roosts to have their young in, and lots and lots of insects to munch on. Some bats even need ponds to drink from and feed over.

You can make sure the bats in your garden have sweet smelling flowers to attract insects. And you can put up a bat box in your garden to make a little shelter for them. You can even put a bat tile on your roof — bats love to live up there, snuggling in the loft.

SUPERFACT
UK bats eat insects like midges, moths and beetles. In summer, a single pipistrelle bat will eat about 3,000 midges a night!

Be a bat detective

Right Batman — er, Super Kid — it's time to get out there and see how many bats you can find in your garden. Trouble is they're practically impossible to spot. So, get yourself what all self-respecting bat detectives need — a bat detector.

This clever little device works by picking up the different high-pitched frequencies that bats use to communicate with each other — usually they are undetectable to the human ear. It then works out what type of bat is in your garden, by listening to the bat voices and matching them up with a type or species of bat. These detectors aren't cheap, but you could form a bat detective group with other Super Kids and pool your pocket money. Or get the Zombie Parents to buy one for your birthday instead!

By all means build a bat house –
but don't get too carried away!

What's it all about, Super Kids? Why bother to save the planet at all? There are two basic reasons. The first is you. Reading this book might make you feel like humans are a waste of space. Perhaps it would have been better if evolution had never invented us? In fact, humans are incredibly amazing creatures. Yes, we have caused all sorts of catastrophes and nightmares for the planet. But most of the time we didn't know what we were doing, until it was too late. It's just taken us a long time to realise how serious some of the problems are.

But humans are capable of acts of extreme kindness, too. Think about Mother Theresa or the Dalai Lama sacrificing themselves for others, the stunning art of Monet and Picasso, incredible structures we have built like the pyramids or beautiful music by composers like Mozart. See, we are not all bad Super Kids. In fact we are a very, very strange mixture between very good and very bad. It's up to you to make the very best of every day of your life. To make yourself into one of the very best humans possible.

The other reason to save the planet is for the others. We share this planet with at least one million other species. One quarter of a million of these are plants. Many of the rest are insects and a few are birds, reptiles and mammals like us. Scientists have only described a tiny fraction of the world's species. It's amazing to think there could be up to 100 million different living things on this planet.

Because of the activities of humans, described in this book, up to 100 of our planet's species are disappearing every day. They are going extinct. Having taken millions of years to evolve into perfect, functional creatures, they are now being blotted out in moments.

And Super Kids, we desperately need these creatures. Ecosystems work because all the different animals and plants have their special places, like pieces inside a computer working to make it function as a whole. Even techy types will tell you, the most sophisticated computers can't measure up to the simplest of living creatures.

Nature is incredibly useful and beautiful. Half of our medicines and all our food comes directly from plants and animals. Ecosystems clean our water and our air, make our soil and absorb our carbon gases. Those animals and plants, considered the lowest of the low like worms, slugs, fungi and bacteria, consume our rubbish and dead bodies. Without them, we would be up to our ears in poo! Such 'natural services' are worth around an estimated £33 trillion a year to the world economy.

Without nature we would not exist at all. Even if we could live on a planet with just other humans and the farmed animals we need to eat, would we want to? When you visit a forest, snorkel in the sea or watch an animal closely, take time to listen to nature and forget yourself. You will feel like you're inside a cathedral, or seeing the most amazing film you've ever watched – only a trillion times better!

Nature inspires artists and poets. It's the origin of all of our favourite characters when we were little, from Pooh Bear to Toad of Toad Hall, *The Lion King* and *Jungle Book*. Animal words are among the first spoken after 'Mummy' and 'Daddy' by kids all over the world. While in the *Children's Book of 1,000 Poems*, around 90% of the poems inside mention animals or plants. Can you imagine a world without animals Super Kids? A world where bears exist only in cartoons. Where tigers live only in history books? Animals are hugely important to our hearts and our minds. We need to make sure they stay happy and safe.

Consider adopting a wild animal

Lots of charities have adopt-an-animal schemes, which allow you to pay for the cost of looking after an animal, without necessarily doing it yourself. This is a good option for eco-heroes living in flats, or those with very busy Zombie Parents who are out at work all day.

Just think, you could be the proud friend of a donkey, a panda or a lion – in fact any animal you admire! Just check out the London Zoo website, www.londonzoo.co.uk/adoptions, where you can adopt any of the wild species they keep.

SUPERFACT
An estimated 40% of all life in the sea has been destroyed over the last 25 years, as a result of our pollution.

Join the birdwatching brigade

Birds are awesome! With their long beaks and delicate wings they are swords in flight, elvish creatures. They can also be as hard as nails and strong as trucks. Super Kids can take inspiration from super-birds. Can you imagine being as small as a sparrow and surviving the British winter? It's freezing out there and yet they exist with only tiny feathers to

protect them, never coming in from the cold to drink a hot chocolate or sit by a radiator.

Meanwhile, some birds travel 1,000s of miles with no map, no car, no aeroplane, no luggage and no passport just to get somewhere warmer for winter! It's called migration. These birds return to the same spot every year, thanks to an inbuilt navigation system, that's even better than a military satellite positioning system!

Yep, birds are really amazing. Want to find out some more? Best thing to do is get yourself some binoculars and go birdwatching.

Finding out about birds from a guidebook is
a very good idea – as long as you don't forget
to watch the creatures themselves.

Make a wildlife map

Fancy yourself as a bit of an explorer? Why not try making a wildlife map of the area around your home? Just put in one or two buildings and roads as landmarks. Then put in your own symbols for trees, bushes, wildflowers and animals. Don't forget to put a key at the bottom so people know what your symbols mean. By looking at the map, your friends will be able to visit all the wildlife near your home too – just like a mini nature trail!

SUPERFACT

Feel like you're living in an urban jungle? Every day we lose over 800 square miles of wildland in the world, as we build over it.

Body-clock rock

With the global weather system changing so quickly, the body-clocks of lots of animals and plants are getting confused. Some even wake up earlier in the year, thinking that spring has come. The scary thing is, the animals and plants that really depend on each other are now getting out of synch. Blue tits need to hatch their young at exactly the right time of year, so they can catch and feed them the right kind of caterpillar. If they time it wrong, the chicks will miss out on their vital dinner. You can see if the climate is changing for yourself by watching the seasons come and go. Help collect the information that finally persuades governments to take real action on global warming – see www.naturedetectives.org.uk.

Support a conservation charity

Conservation charities go out into the world and work with wild animals in their natural habitat. You can support them by organising fundraising events at school. Some charities also give you the chance to sponsor a wild animal and keep track of how it's getting along out there. Sponsor a turtle at www.archelon.gr and www.watamuturtle.com, a humpback whale at www.iwc.org, or a chimpanzee at www.ida-africa.org. Or help save our woodlands and endangered species like the Iberian lynx (a type of wild cat), at www.siren.org.uk.

Some flowers are blooming earlier in the year than ever before because of climate change – sometimes even in the winter.

Shhhh

Hush now!

When someone enters your home, they must respect your space and not steal your toys or damage your house. It's the same when you go into nature. Remember Super Kids, when you enter the world of the forest, the mountain or the country park, you are in someone else's home. The home of creatures totally different to ourselves.

Listen! You will hear birdsong. Which bird is singing? What are they saying? Why do they sing like that all day? Can you hear a grasshopper rubbing together its back legs, speaking to other grasshoppers in a strange language, like an alien creature in the grass? What's that above? A kestrel or a sparrowhawk hunting for small mammals in the grass? With X-ray vision they spot their prey, creatures that scurry through the undergrowth, leaving trails of scent to let their friends – and enemies – know exactly where they are. Sometimes it's fun just to play in the forest or park and make noise, build dens, climb trees and scramble around getting muddy. But sometimes, Super Kids, listen and look into the other world – you won't be disappointed.

SUPERFACT

There are now more than 21,000 species of animal that are threatened or endangered around the world.

Get a guidebook

There are loads of field guides, which can help eco-detectives in the countryside work out who is walking over their boot, creeping in the undergrowth or singing from the bushes. You can buy bird guides, beetle guides, worm guides, mushroom guides, flower guides, bug guides, tree guides – pretty much any kind of guide to help reveal the names and homes of different species living in all parts of the world. The more you know about the rest of the world's creatures, the more you will want to help them. For starters, it's only polite to know their names!

Get to know what you're looking at. It's fun, it's
interesting – and it might turn out to be important.

Get out your torch

Nature comes alive at night-time too. Flying
through our starry skies, whistling and hunting
through our trees are the Harry Potter owls and
bats. These creatures of magic, myth and legend are
relatively easy to see, as long as you have a torch. Take
a rechargeable one (that uses energy from the mains) and
creep out into the darkness, with parent in tow for double the fun.

Adopt a bat

No eco-hero is complete without a bat detector, as you'll also read in the
Garden section. These amazing little black boxes can listen into the world
of bats, translate what they say and change the sound so humans can
hear it too. Each of the different bat species in Britain makes a different
call. You can tell which is which by listening in with your hi-tech bat box.
But did you know you can also adopt a bat, too? Bat World rescues
injured or captured bats, and puts them up for adoption. You can visit
their website at www.batworld.org.

SUPERFACT

Plants have been used since ancient
times, as treatments and cures. Part of the
purple foxglove is still used for treating
heart conditions – while a drug made partly
from the rosy periwinkle of Madagascar, is
used to treat childhood leukaemia.

Quick, hide!

To get to know wild animals you have be quiet and sit still. Animals are
not used to humans. In fact, because we are often dangerous they tend
to avoid us. You can build a hide out of sticks and leaves, perhaps at
the base of tree. You have to be patient and let animals come along and
carry on their lives around you. Maybe a deer will walk right past, or even
a badger. Badgers have brilliant noses but they're shortsighted. So as
long as you sit still and stay downwind, you can hide by their sett and
they won't see or smell you!

All you need to 'go bats' is a good torch and some
fellow bat-watchers to go out into the night with.
Take a parent with you, too.

Fancy a spot of wolf-watching?

Super Kids, do you really want to sit on a beach this holiday watching your mum turn into a bacon crisp – or would you rather spend it singing to the wolves up a mountain? Fancy a trip to Butlins – or would you prefer to plant enough trees to house 100 red squirrels? Bored with basketball for the 258th time? How about counting turtles on a Greek Island? There are loads of ways to be an eco-volunteer and make a difference during your holiday. Look in BBC Wildlife magazine for ideas.

Wise up on wildlife

If wildlife fascinates you, then become a real expert. Start by reading the *Encyclopedia of Mammals by David Macdonald and Sasha Norris*, which tells you all about all the world's furries. Or any of the amazing books on the world's other creeping, flying, swooping creatures.

SUPERFACT

Big isn't always powerful. Elephants, with an African population of 1,450,000 in the 1980s are now down to 500,000. The blue whale, the biggest animal ever, may now be down to just 10,000. The five species of rhino, at fewer than 12,400 animals, could actually disappear in 30 years.

Beachcombing

Leave the shells where they lie on the beach, Super Kids. You never know when a hermit crab might come along. These creatures make their homes inside the cast-off shells of other marine animals. As they grow, they shuffle out of the old homes and need to find a new shell to live in. A bit like you, when you grow out of your clothes. But beachcombing can still be brilliant fun. Just follow the golden rule – it's fine to take anything man-made that washes up, just avoid the natural stuff. This includes shells, coral and pebbles, as these are all part of Mother Nature's grand plan and she needs them.

You can learn loads about wildlife from books. You can find out a fair bit from your Mum and Dad, too!

Go on a fungal foray

Every year in our woodlands, some curious beings from the underworld emerge and show their strange selves. They are neither animal nor plant. They don't need light to live. Instead they hide, silent and deadly in soil, old tree stumps and even living branches, creeping like a plague. What are they? The mushrooms and toadstools – or fungi – that live all around us.

Fungi aren't all bad. They are nature's recyclers, eating away at anything they can push themselves into. They travel between homes using tiny microscopic spores, so small they can't be seen by the human eye. They land on an old tree or dead body and slip in to eat away from the inside out. Then every autumn, our woods come alive with evidence that they exist.

There are thousands of different types of fungi. Some are delicious to eat and are sold for very high prices in expensive restaurants. Others are poisonous and have been used in famous murders. So know your fungi Super Kids – you never know when you might have to solve a murder!

Be zoo aware

In Britain over 400,000 animals live in cages in zoos, far from their homes and natural habitat. So what do they get out of it? Ideally, they're helping in conservation. Good zoos learn all they can from captive creatures to help their relatives in the wild. Some animals need caring for by zoos before they can be sent back home safely. Meanwhile breeding programmes in other zoos can also help endangered species survive.

Like humans, animals deserve good living quarters too. Some zoos provide the most boring living spaces, which makes the animals unhappy. Be critical if you visit a zoo. Does the chimp look as if it's got enough toys to play with? Is the gorilla sad or is it hanging out with friends? How big is the wolf cage? Visit www.zoowatch.freeserve.co.uk/ and the *Good Zoo Guide* at www.goodzoos.com/ to check out zoos near you.

Each year in our woodlands, curious fungi emerge from the underworld and show their strange selves.

Make way for Madame Butterfly

Make a home for butterflies and their caterpillars in your garden. There are a few dozen of them resident in Britain and six or so that visit us regularly from abroad. They have babies if the conditions are right. And many of them love to munch on plants in your garden.

Don't kill off these caterpillars with chemicals. Encourage them and you will have their elflike parents flying through your little patch every year. The caterpillars of many of the loveliest garden butterflies, like peacocks and tortoiseshells, feed on nettles. These plants are nasty stingers to humans — but the perfect snack for these potential festive flitters!

Give them a home and a healthy meal. Let a corner of your garden go wild with nettles and watch the spikey, black babies emerge and grow.

SUPERFACT
There are 56 native species of butterfly currently living in the UK, including the recently re-introduced Large Blue. Since 1,800, four others have become extinct.

Go butterfly watching

Super Kids, venture beyond your garden. Find butterflies that have come here from abroad too. The beautiful Queen of Spain fritillary butterfly is a common visitor to Britain and Ireland. Its wings have an angular shape with large silver patches below, which make it really distinctive. Good news for budding butterfly spotters — sightings have increased in recent years. Let's hope they're here to stay.

Or look out for the Monarch. This large and striking butterfly is famous for its migrations from North America to Mexico. Sometimes it even crosses the Atlantic to reach Europe. Some years are better than others in Britain and Ireland, but sightings are increasing all the time. To find out more visit www.butterfly-conservation.org.

Encourage plants in your garden, and you should have
butterflies all through the summer months.

Get to know the Ancient countryside

In 3500 BC, early farmers lived in a place where two-thirds of the country was covered by trees. In 1086 AD, the Domesday Book showed that only 20 per cent of England was still covered with trees. Sadly, the last 1,000 years have also seen several native animals become extinct in Britain. In our quest for building materials, hunting for food and sport, and places to live – which have destroyed much of our natural habitat – we have helped cause the extinction of the brown bear, the aurochs (a type of wild ox), the beaver, the wild boar and the wolf, all by the end of the 18th century!

Otters have suffered at our hands too. When farmers began to use pesticides in the 1950s, otters saw a sudden crash in numbers. These pesticides were washed into rivers and worked their way up the food-chain, either killing the otters or affecting their breeding and resistance to disease. Much of Britain's wildlife is making a comeback – otters, big birds of prey, even wild boar are snuffling around in our woods. And tree planting schemes are turning our landscape back into the forest-clad land of yore. Find out more from The Mammal Society, PlantLife, the Wildlife Trusts, and Siren at www.siren.org.uk.

SUPERFACT
Over the past 45 years, a quarter of our hedgerows have been destroyed, at a rate of about 4,000 miles a year!

How old is that hedge?

1. Choose a 30 metre length of hedge.
2. Count the number of species of trees and shrubs you find in it.
3. Multiply that number by 100, to find the hedge's age in years.

If you think a really old hedge with lots of wildlife living in it is about to be destroyed, you might be able to stop it by contacting the Tree Officer at your district or county council. Act now!

It's amazing what you can find in and around
old hedges. Grasshoppers, crickets and sometimes
even old cricket balls!

Don't snooze in biology

Want to live a really wild life, having adventures with wild animals in the Arctic or desert, exploring the world's most far out places or living alongside tigers, elephants or bears? The trick is to make sure you read as much as possible, pay attention in biology and leave school with the right knowledge and skills to take you into the wilderness.

Want to help look after our animals? Lots of people have jobs in this field, trying to make sure our endangered creatures don't disappear forever. If that's what you really want to do, stay informed and just keep believing in your dream. It can come true!

Let nature take its course

It's spring, you're out for a walk and you find a baby bird that can't fly properly yet, all alone on the ground. Do you take it home with you to look after it? The answer is no. If there's a cat nearby, move the bird carefully to a safer place. Otherwise leave the baby bird for its mum. She's probably watching nearby and simply waiting for you to leave.

SUPERFACT

One of the worst oil slicks to hit the UK was in 1993. The Braer tanker hit some rocks and spilt 85,000 tonnes of oil over 400km of coastline. About 30,000 sea birds were killed.

Support marine conservation

Between January 1971 and June 1979, 36,000 birds were found dead around the British coast, covered in oil from sea tankers and cars. Go and do something about marine pollution Super Kids. Visit the Marine Conservation Society at www.mcsuk.org.

If you want a career in conservation or natural history,
keep yourself informed – and keep living the dream.

Plant a tree to fight pollution

Trees are so brilliant, they can even solve one of our silliest errors – they absorb nasty gases like carbon dioxide. These are released by human activities and are one of the main causes of global warming. Super Kids, we can help soak up these carbon emissions by keeping our forests alive!

How? If you fly to Spain on a Jumbo 747 for your holidays, your plane uses 137kg of fuel. This is as much energy as the electricity of three 60 watt light bulbs lit continuously, or the food eaten by two people in one year. Broken down, this makes you responsible for 1,278kg of carbon dioxide in the atmosphere. Plant some trees to absorb the gases your aeroplane gives off – in this case the equivalent of a tree ten feet tall – and make your holiday carbon neutral. Or better still, don't fly at all!

5 more great reasons to hug a tree

Trees are central to the business of saving the world. They are also some of the most interesting things on the planet. Here are the facts:

1. Two thirds of all the animals in the world live inside trees and forests.

2. Trees provide us with warmth from firewood, charcoal and coal, shelter from building materials and the sun, plus fruit, nuts, cork, broomsticks, magic wands, furniture and fishing rods.

3. Without trees, our ancestors would not have been able to travel across water in their wooden boats.

4. Trees bind soil so that other plants can live on the forest floor. All types of creatures, like tree frogs, woodpeckers, bats and spiders live in them.

5. Trees are the oldest things on the planet, some getting on for 1,500 years old. That's even older than Gandalf!

The more we use aeroplanes to travel, the more we need
trees to absorb the carbon dioxide they give off.
So reduce flying and get planting today!

Plant a tree by the road

Clever roadside trees can absorb pollution directly from cars that are travelling from place to place. They also absorb noise so that the road is not so grumpy. Find out more about tree-planting and how it can help protect the world, from the Tree Council at www.treecouncil.org.uk.

SUPERFACT

On average, planting five trees can off-set the harmful emissions from driving a car 12,000 miles.

Join the Woodcraft folk

Wanna go wild, ramble in the woods, learn to look after trees, make campfires and climb in the canopy? Contact www.woodcraft.org.uk for action-packed adventures outside. After a week of mountain-biking, stream-scrambling, map-reading and even some serious conservation work with fellow eco-heroes, you won't want to come home!

Save the rainforest!

In 1987, an area of the Amazon rainforest the size of Britain was burned, adding 500 million tonnes of carbon dioxide to the atmosphere. Every minute an estimated 80 football pitches of rainforest are destroyed. The loss of these forests means fewer trees are left to absorb carbon dioxide and replenish oxygen supplies. While burning wood is better for the world than burning fossil fuel like coal, we need to put back what we take. This is called sustainable planting. Find out more by reading the Focus on Forests section at www.worldlandtrust.org.

Planting a tree by the side of the road can help
absorb pollution from nearby traffic. Just make
sure you get permission first.

Toys

Toys, as all Super Kids know, are brilliant. Where would we be without them? Nowhere, that's where! Toys are part of having fun, growing up and finding out about life – and everyone's got their favourites.

All animals in the world use toys and games, to make learning how to be a grown-up more fun. Young penguins spend their time sliding down icebergs into the sea to practice their swimming and gain physical strength, lion cubs play chase to learn to hunt and elephant kids often look after baby elephants to learn how to be good mothers. If you play games that teach you about the world we live in, when you grow up, you'll be able to work in a more interesting way.

But sometimes, it's the things we love the most that we have to be super careful about. Super Kids need to be very thoughtful when it comes to buying new toys and gadgets. That's because lots of toys use up the world's valuable resources.

The world population is massively on the increase. Every second, on average five people are born, and the global population is doubling every 40 years. If everyone in the world lived like we do, we'd need six planets to sustain us. That's because there just aren't enough resources like trees, oil and water to make the things we demand. Everything we buy or do, uses up resources that cost the earth something. It's really important that Super Kids think, before they pester their parents for new toys.

New toys and games can use up the world's resources.
Why not get what you want from a toy library instead?

RED ALERT! WORLD GONE MAD WARNING!

Batteries, Super Kids, are little bombs of pollution waiting to go off as soon as they have left your grasp. They explode with chemicals that trickle out into the soil and make the world a smellier, dirtier place. Normal batteries should be a thing of the past — shoved into museum display cases and laughed at. That's how bad batteries are for the planet. So do your best to get rid of them. Only buy toys that don't need them.

Here comes the sun

If you really need batteries eco-kids, buy solar-powered, rechargeable ones. Just park them on your windowsill or anywhere under the sun, and recharge using a completely eco-friendly power. Don't you just love the sun?

SUPERFACT

The average household uses 21 batteries a year, but only a small percentage of them are recycled. Most end up on landfill sites where their heavy metals leak into the soil, causing water and soil pollution, which endangers wildlife.

Recharge your batteries

Super Kids, you can stop the madness! Is your walkman sounding weary? Is your Nintendo getting needy? Ask your parents to feed them up again, with rechargeable batteries. These brilliant things can be plugged into the wall socket and charged up, over and over again — which means you get to use battery-powered toys whenever you want. Not quite as good as solar powered, but there will always be a ready supply of energy at home.

Turn your toys into sun-worshippers too, by reviving
their batteries with a solar-powered device.

Share the fun

Super Kids, are you harbouring old toys, letting them loiter and litter up your bedroom? Is your attic packed with old dolls, games or Lego, no longer loved by YOU?

Give these toys a new lease of life – send them to a child who really needs or wants them. All over the world there are children who come from families that can't afford to buy toys. You can make their lives shinier and happier, by passing on your old toys, today.

There are lots of charities who will pass on your old or unwanted toys. If you're not sure where to send them, the list of websites on the right should get you started.

Looking for a charity that gives your old toys to someone who really needs or wants them? Try:

www.oxfam.org.uk

www.barnardos.org.uk

www.savethechildren.org.uk

www.samaritanspurse.org

Make wood work

Wooden toys, made from renewable forests are the best you can buy. They will disappear into nothing when released into the world. When these toys are made, they also do less harm to the planet. See what fun you can have at www.woodentoys-uk.co.uk.

Keep toys safe

When your toys escape on the beach or in the park, where do they end up – littering the seabed or being eaten by a bird? Most toys are made from plastic, with loads of colourful chemicals locked inside. When they escape into nature, the sun gets to work melting the plastic and releasing poisons onto the earth or into the atmosphere. Animals and plants don't like it. So make sure your toys never end up polluting the world – take them home at the end of the day!

**Don't let your toys escape.
You never know where they might end up!**

Wild at heart?

Once upon a time, Super Kids, humans lived dangerous lives. There wasn't always enough food and water to go around. People would come from other villages to steal. If necessary they'd kill, because if they didn't they might die of starvation. Wild animals were dangerous too. They lived all around us and we didn't have doors to keep them out. Lots of kids died before they could grow up. Today, of course life is not like that, but inside all of us, a little bit of prehistoric kid lives on. Somewhere deep down, we think our enemies are still out to steal our food. That's why we play aggressive games and watch aggressive films – even though we don't need to. You can help change this Super Kids, by using your powers of protection instead of aggression.

SUPERFACT

Research in the US has shown that one in five children are affected by violence on TV. Children brought up to think violence is OK, are more likely to turn into the playground bully or even become a criminal!

Avoid war games

Do you play with toys that pretend to maim and destroy? Are you shooting guns at your friends or do you spend all day zapping your enemy? Are you toys turning you into an eco-demon? Wars and guns are real. They hurt people and they hurt their parents. The people in wars are just like you and just like your Mum and Dad. Except these kids end up with no homes or families. Guns make people miserable and lead terrible lives. Guns are not for playing with. Find out more from www.lionlamb.org.

SUPERFACT

Half the world's engineers and physicists work exclusively on weapons development. Meanwhile, every year, the world spends more than £1000 billion on weapons and the military. That's a lot of war!

Build an army with a difference.
See what your imagination can come up with!

Watch out for Phthalates!

Sometimes, Super Kids need to get technical. Sometimes, chemistry can help Super Kids save the world. Plastic toys contain phthalates, which are nasty chemicals believed to – WAIT FOR IT SUPER KIDS – damage your testicles or ovaries before you are even born! These phthalates can also cause cancer in kids playing with the toys or very poor workers around the world who make them. Wooden toys are much kinder to the environment and last longer, too. Find them through **www.smallworldtoys.co.uk** or contact the British Toy Makers Guild at **www.toymakersguild.co.uk**.

SUPERFACT
A woman working at a factory in Haiti, sewing cartoon t-shirts, can handle about 375 shirts an hour – but she only earns 20p in this time. To buy back one of those t-shirts would cost her a full week's wages!

All the fun of the fair

While you're having fun, Super Kids, you need to make sure that no one else is suffering. Over 100 million children in the world are forced to work so people in the west have things to buy. These kids should be learning things in school – not making footballs in factories! Some of these people are so poor and desperate for money, they take any work offered, by people from rich countries like Britain or America. Often they take them at the lowest possible salaries. That means the rich people stay rich – and the poor people stay poor. No money means no food, which sometimes leaves them too tired, ill or weak to work. It's a vicious cycle.

So choose Fairtrade. This is a way of making sure people don't get exploited in this way, and everyone earns a decent amount of money for their work. Then they can afford to send their children to school and buy good food. Get clued up on Fairtrade at **www.traidcraft.co.uk**.

Over 100 million children in the world
are working to make things like t-shirts and
footballs, for people in the west to buy.

Are you a computer game geek?

Do you like playing on the latest computer game more than meeting friends? Computer geek alert! Computer games can be good fun, but Super Kids, if you spend hours on them, you might struggle to mix easily with friends in future years. You could also develop nasty aches and pains from sitting in the same position, day after day. If you must play on, make it easier on yourself by following these top five tips:

1. It takes two
Two-player games can be far more fun and keep you chatting. It's hard to keep quiet, when your friend pulls a cheeky move and takes the lead!

2. Break it up
No one can sit and do the same task for hours without getting zombified. And you don't want to end up like your Zombie Parents!

3. And stretch
Get up and have a stretch. Or get a glass of water or a cup of Fairtrade tea. Your eyes need time to adjust from staring at the screen.

4. Thumbs up
Simple thumb movements include clenching and unclenching your fist and flexing your fingers. Remember your hands need a break too.

5. Tomorrow is another day
Don't set yourself impossible tasks. The game will still be there tomorrow! Go out and take some exercise in the fresh air instead.

SUPERFACT
A recent survey showed more than 80% of kids under six years old watch up to six hours of TV every day! And a third play video games too.

Go fly your kite

Up in the air Super Kids, your kite takes flight and carries your dreams. Flying a kite is brilliant fun – and good news for Super Kids, you can do it without anything bad happening to the planet. Visit www.planetplay.co.uk

Kite-flying is a great way to spend an afternoon.
You can make your kite out of old paper, too.

Join a toy library

Toy libraries are great ways of saving money and the earth. You can borrow what you want for a week or two, then take it back and get a new toy. Contact the National Association of Toy and Leisure Libraries on 0208 7387 9592 or visit their website at www.natl.org.uk.

Defend your playing field

Super Kids, escape the Zombie Parents with a trip to the playing fields. There you can run, jump, skate, lounge around chatting, have a picnic, make snowmen in winter, and most of all have fun. But be warned Super Kids. Every day, a playing field is concreted over to make new offices that probably won't be used anyway. Your playing field is your green space, so don't let them steal it! The National Playing Fields Association are true eco-heroes, trying to save these spaces. Visit them at www.npfa.co.uk.

SUPERFACT
Approximately 5,000 playing fields were lost to new development between 1987 and 1997.

Mark out your HQ

All super-heroes need a headquarters to hide in – a secret place to discuss matters of extreme importance to the planet. Using old sheets and chairs you can set up a secret den in your bedroom. Make it as secure as possible. And make sure that no one comes in without the 'secret code'. There are loads of ways to play without having to BUY ANYTHING AT ALL. Super Kids, experiment with having fun!

Sew your support

Why not make dolls and toys from old clothes. That way you get exactly the design you want, that's totally unique! Have a look at the Blue Peter website for great ideas at www.bbc.co.uk/cbbc/bluepeter/make.

Set up your HQ – it's amazing what you can build out of old bits and pieces in the privacy of your own room!

The way that most of us use fossil fuels is by racing around in our cars. Every year 65 million new cars are made in the world, but there are 500 million already puffing about. The trouble is, they release carbon gases to destroy the fantastically complex global weather patterns that support life on earth. Sitting in cars also makes us fatter and less fit. Be wise, Super Kids and tell your Zombie Parents too. There are better, more world-saving ways to get about, than the gas-guzzlers we are used to hopping into everyday. To show you how, answer this simple quiz.

You're late for school, which is only about a mile away. Which is the best option of transport for you to take?

⇨   persuading your mum to give you a lift in the car
⇨   going on your bike
⇨   walking
⇨   taking the bus
⇨   pulling a sicky because it's too embarrassing to be late AGAIN!

If you take the day off, you'll be in even bigger trouble tomorrow! Getting Mum or Dad to drive is the lazy option – at 8.56am it probably won't be that quick anyway, because of rush-hour traffic. The bus will be stuck all the way too, even with bus-lanes, because of all that traffic. In eco-terms, the best solution is walking or biking. You could be late – but CHOOSE THE BIKE AND JUMP ON SUPER KIDS! It's worth it to save the world.

Remember, cars are also powered by petrol, which is a fossil fuel. It ignites when you turn on the engine. This releases nasty gases from eco-enemy fossil fuels into the air, causing funny weather and a smelly, dirty world. Cars alone generate around 5% of the carbon emission to the atmosphere.

How to lose friends and mess up the atmosphere:
get Mum to give you a lift to school.

Only use your car, if you're going far

Half of all car journeys made are under two miles. In the morning at 8.50am, one in five cars contains imprisoned school kids, slowly being poisoned by the air pollution inside the car. Carbon monoxide at very high doses can kill you because it joins with your blood instead of oxygen. Then you run out of energy. Carbon monoxide is eight times higher inside a car, than in normal outside air! Two miles takes half an hour to walk and 10 minutes to cycle. You arrive fitter, brighter, breezier and ready for action.

SUPERFACT

Cars spend an average of 44 days a year stuck in traffic. In Bangkok there are long periods every day when the traffic moves at only 3 km an hour. You can walk faster than that!

On the double

If you live miles from anywhere and really do need to use a car to get to school or see friends, try to car-share. Maybe there are other children in your village who go to the same school as you. If not, maybe you could do a round trip. This will also save your Zombie Parents some precious time and less time stuck in traffic jams might help them feel less zombified!

SUPERFACT

There are 10 million empty car seats on our roads, clogging up our streets. That's because 60% of all journeys happen with only one person in the car.

Turn off your engine

If Mum or Dad are sat still in a traffic jam for more than two minutes, get them to turn off the engine. There's no point killing the planet if you're not going anywhere.

Every time you jump into the car, you start
yet another grim journey for the world.

Go anywhere on your bike

There are cycle paths all over the country, Super Kids. With some maps and a bit of planning you can get just about everywhere. You can even pack a rucksack and go camping on your bike. Contact www.sustrans.org to find out how.

SUPERFACT

In 2005, there were no less than 10,000 miles of National Cycle Network. If you stretched them all out together, they'd reach all the way from Britain to Australia!

Notch it up a gear

Cycling is also a great way of keeping fit and healthy, and building up your strength to save the planet. Today's bikes are a great help with all those gears. Instead of just coasting along though, try notching up a gear on the flat. That way you'll steadily increase your stamina and find pedal-power you never even knew you had!

Love your bike

Bikes need oiling, their brakes checked and their tyres pumped up. They also enjoy life best if they're kept under cover. When riding your bike always wear a super-hero helmet and a brightly coloured jacket. If you can get a fluorescent yellow one, all the better to let the mad Zombie Drivers know you're coming through.

Organise a fundraiser to get a school mini-bus

The next stage in the global warrior's fight for a green planet is to bring your community together to buy a school minibus. A litre of petrol will carry one person, four miles in a large car. In a minibus, the same amount of petrol will carry 40 passengers a whole 31 miles. You need to recruit more Super Kids and several Zombie Parents if you're going to achieve a minibus for your school. You never know, the Zombies might just wake up to undertake this mission with you. If anyone says you're being unreasonable, remind them that change depends on people wanting it. For more information on eco-friendly transport, contact www.eta.co.uk.

There are cycle paths all over the country, and with some careful planning you can get just about anywhere.

Park and Ride

Don't let Mum or Dad go blue in the face, sitting in another traffic jam on the way to town on Saturday. Get them to park and ride. These nifty little systems mean you can park your car in a ready-made car park at the edge of town and then jump on a bus. The bus then bombs along the bus lanes all the way to the town centre without your parents having to get road-rage on the way. It also saves everyone else in town from your fumes, and you from Mum or Dad's fuming! In fact, someone worked out that car fumes are so high on a busy day in Oxford, you may as well be smoking 184 cigarettes a day – not such a good idea, especially when you're a kid!

Let the train take the strain

Travelling by train is much more energy-efficient than going in a car. It's more fun, you get to talk to your Zombie Parents who are not taken up with getting lost and getting cross. Most importantly, railways take up MUCH LESS SPACE! Thirty thousand people can be carried around by railway every hour, while roads carry only 10% of this amount. A train releases far less carbon monoxide than a car, too.

Write to your council

Request car-free streets and zones where you can play safely with your friends. KIDS ARE MORE IMPORTANT THAN CARS! Let the world know. To find out how, see the section on campaigning later in this book.

SUPERFACT
Petrol fumes contain carbon monoxide, carbon dioxide, nitrogen oxide, soot, oil vapour and lead – all potentially dangerous to human health.

Going by train is much more energy-efficient than going in a car. You can get to see some fantastic views as you travel, too.

Organise a local car-free day campaign

Why not get a load of your mates to walk to school together? You can plan a route and pick each other up on the way. You'll have to make sure you've got directions and that you leave early enough to be on time! There's even an organisation that can help you plan your walk to school at www.iwalktoschool.org.

Pick up the pace

Did you know, every day most of us take between 3,000 and 4,000 steps? Sounds like a lot? Well, actually it's not enough. Experts say we should aim for 10,000 steps a day, to maintain a healthy lifestyle. Walking with a pedometer can help make this more fun. This clever and quite cheap little gadget, calculates how many steps you take as you walk along. You attach it to your waistband and it does the counting! Start by finding out how many steps you take each day, then set goals to increase your total.

Kestrel count

Next time you're travelling down the motorway, don't waste time car-spotting, keep an eye out for birds of prey. Kestrels are a common sight along Britain's motorways. You can watch them hover and swoop on voles and mice hiding in the embankments. You can't miss them once you know what you're looking for, and, if you're lucky you'll spot one dive-bombing its prey!

SUPERFACT
In Britain, there are nearly 30 million vehicles.

Go on an eco-holiday

Family holidays can cost the earth. For distances under 500 kilometres, an aeroplane makes three times as much carbon dioxide and pollution as going by rail. Get your family to travel by boat or train. It's much more exciting, as you get to look at scenery on the way. Visit www.seat61.com for how to get around without leaving the ground!

SUPERFACT
In Europe, three times as many people die from the bad effects of air pollution from cars, than die in car accidents.

You don't have to holiday by car or plane. Try a more eco-friendly form of transport. It's better for the planet, and you'll probably find you see much more, too.

Having Fun

A Super Kid's life shouldn't all be about protecting the world. What's the point in saving the planet if you can't go out and enjoy it? And there's loads to get super-excited about – if you just know where to look.

The big green, grassy, wet countryside is fun, free and not too far away! It's like one massive playground. And you can use your super-detection skills to learn about wildlife and further your mission to help it. Check out **www.wildlifetrusts.org** to see what's in your area. If you fancy getting even closer to animals, then have a look at www.country-side-explorer.com for Animal Farms. If you've always wanted to cuddle a woolly lamb or a squealing baby piglet, check one out. If you live in a city, there are fabulous farmyard antics, right on your doorstep too, in City Farms.

Meanwhile, what happens when you get in from school? Open a bag of crisps, a tin of soft drink and sit down in front of the telly? There you are, far off the track of saving the planet. You gotta get up and go and do something more interesting. Something which will make you an asset to the global population of Super Kids. After-school clubs can sometimes be pretty dull. But you can set the agenda, just by going along. They are there for you, Super Kids. Take a copy of the Super Kids manual for fixing the planet – this book – and you will find a ready made mob of kids to put up bat boxes, lobby parliament or make Christmas cards with. And you may find that things are more interesting than you thought. Excited already? Check out **www.clubsforyoungpeople.org.uk**, to find one near you.

Get outdoors – it's the place to be.

Escape the Zombie Parents!

It's that time of year again – the summer holidays! Hurrah! Weeks of no homework and having fun with your friends. No school is great, but don't you ever get bored with all those weeks off? True Super Kids are always up for new challenges and learning new things. So, why not suggest to your parents you go on a summer camp? These are special camps that run through the summer, where you can try loads of fun activities, parent-free! From archery to orienteering and canoeing, there's plenty to have a go at. There are tonnes of summer camps up and down the country – ask your school to see if they have a link to one near you. Or have a look at www.pgl.co.uk and www.campbeaumont.com.

SUPERFACT

Britain has 14 National Parks. These include some of the most remote and dramatic landscapes of England, Scotland and Wales, from sweeping heather moorlands, to dramatic coastlines and breath-taking uplands and mountains.

Learning for fun

If the great outdoors is not right on your doorstep, get your Zombie Parents out on a day-trip. There are conservation and education centres all over the UK, just check out http://www.schoolgovernment.co.uk/FSC/FSC.htm. You can get your hands dirty digging around in the mud and sand and learning about the others – the creatures who live alongside us in the British Isles. Ideal for Super Kids, and even better for Zombie Parents who haven't felt the sand between their toes for years. Remind them that they're never to old to learn!

Get kitted out

To enjoy being out in the countryside, you must have the right Super Kid outfit. Don't let your enthusiastic but ever so impractical Dad drag you though winter in a flimsy dress and silly shoes (that goes for the boys too!). You need solid hiking boots and warm woollies covered with waterproofs. Then it doesn't matter how bad the weather is, you can always have fun.

Get yourself kitted out – it's all about having the right gear for the right place.

Have yourself a green Christmas!

At Christmas we go into an all-consuming, all-disposing frenzy – and our concerns for the environment get thrown out of the window. No one likes a Scrooge and it's great to give and receive in return. But before you go consumer crazy, stop and think about what you're buying. There could be an eco-friendly alternative just down the page.

Say it on recycled

About 1.7 billion cards get sent in Britain every year. It takes 200,000 trees to make this many cards. These trees are happily growing in Rudolph's garden, providing homes for insects, birds and all sorts of wildlife. If you want to add to the pile of Christmas cards, make sure you send recycled ones. You can buy 'green cards' at www.thegreencardcompany.co.uk. And if you get them from www.woodland-trust.org.uk or www.treesforlife.org.uk, you'll be helping save our trees and woodlands too.

SUPERFACT
It's estimated more than 83 square metres of wrapping paper ends up in UK bins every Christmas. Enough to cover Guernsey or Hyde Park in London, three times over!

Find a safe deposit box

You can also take any cards you receive, to the Woodland Trust recycling points in WH Smith or Tesco.

Make your own

Why not use last year's cards to make new ones? Be creative with scissors and cut shapes out of the front of cards, then write on the back. Or use stickers to cover up the writing and add your own message on top. You can make great labels for presents cheaply and ecologically this way. Amazing home-made decorations can also be made from recycled and scrap paper – old newspapers and junk mail make great paper-chains. And sweet papers can be used to make really pretty tree ornaments. You could even theme them, Super Kids, to show what you've been up to this year – from saving animals to recycling.

It's amazing what you can use to create your
home-made Christmas decorations.

Get sticking

It's easy to reuse old envelopes again with stickers from charities like Oxfam and Friends of the Earth. With the label carrying the name of the charity, you're also helping to tell the world about their good work.

Do the charity thing

Save the world while you shop – make sure you buy things that are made with respect for others and harmony in mind. Oxfam have a brilliant selection of toys. Buying second-hand clothes or books as gifts is a great way to recycle too. Anything that gives something back to this planet is a global eco-warrior's first choice.

SUPERFACT
Every Christmas we throw away enough rubbish to fill **400,000** double decker buses. That's enough to stretch all the way from London to New York!

Make someone else's Christmas

Join a national surge for good, by joining other Super Kids in giving their toys to people who really need them. The thing about growing up is that you grow out of your old toys, too. But loads of kids would love to get their hands on your cast-offs. Especially kids whose parents are poor.

All you need to do is collect any old toys, through the year, in a shoe box. In November, add a couple of sweeties, some paper, crayons and a photo of yourself – that way the kid can see what 'Santa' looks like. Put a note on the box, saying whether it's for a boy or a girl, and roughly what age you think it would suit. Then take it to your nearest Kwik-Fit or hand it in at another special collection point. From there, it will be whisked off abroad and given to a child who will really love it. For more info on recycling toys visit www.samaritanspurse.org. Or see the Toy section for more people who can help.

A shoebox full of your old toys makes a great present
for children in poorer countries.

OK Super Kids, now you're armed with the knowledge and the ideas, you're ready to get out there and save the planet. There's just one thing left to do – take a look in the mirror.

No super-hero can tackle the world's problems, until he or she is good and ready – and that goes for Super Kids too. If you're not looking after yourself properly, then you won't be at the peak of your powers. And let's face it, Super Kids, the world needs you to be fighting fit.

So how do you find out if you're ready to save the world? Super Kids, it's time to take the Dirty Dozen Challenge!

Starting on the next page, there are 12 questions about you, each with a yes or no answer. Read each question fully, then tick your answer in the box by the side (and you gotta be honest, Super Kids!) Then find out your score from the chart at the end.

Super Kids, it's over to you . . .

**The Super Kids are waiting for you to join.
Take this test to find out if you're ready!**

THE DIRTY DOZEN
HOW DO YOU SCORE?

I. DO YOU . . .

Eat too much sugar?
YES ☑ NO ☑ *sometimes*

Once upon a time, sugar was very rare in the world. For millions of years, humans had to eat the things that lived alongside them in the forests. In prehistoric times, we might get to eat honey once a month – or plums once a year, when the trees had fruit on them. Sugar in very small quantities and at certain times can be good for you. It's full of monosaccharides – or simple sugars – that your body finds really easy to turn into instant energy. That's why sugar tastes so good.

But now we have too much. Sugar is so common, because humans learned how to grow sugar cane and get the sugar out. Now, there's so much sugar, it makes us sick – everyone is walking around with brown teeth, fillings and fat. It can even cause serious diseases like diabetes. If you only eat sugar for energy instead of healthy foods, it can leave you very tired and grumpy. Super Kids, don't let sugar cravings get a hold on you!

2. DO YOU . . .

Eat lots of coloured sweets?
YES ☐ NO ☑

E-numbers are the artificial additives pumped into food, for all sorts of reasons, like changing the colour, texture, flavour or to preserve food. Sweets are real baddies, packed full of E-numbers. They might do a great job of making your sweet taste like bananas – but you might also go bananas! After all, E-numbers are chemicals. When we eat them, they will have an effect on us, even if we don't know what that is. Some E-numbers like E110, E124, E122 and E211 can even make people hyperactive – especially kids!

Not great for Super Kids. They need to stay calm and collected if they're gonna save the world. Always check the label on your sweet packet first.

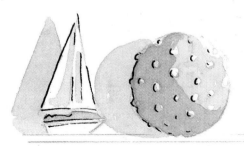

Beware of the possible effects of E-numbers in coloured sweets. They could send you wild!

3. DO YOU . . .

Prefer a fizzy drink to a glass of water?
YES ☐ **NO** ☑

They may taste great, but fizzy drinks are full of sugar and additives, that in time can make you look old and haggard.

Real Super Kids know that drinking lots of water is key to looking good, feeling fit and being ready to save the world. Always make sure you have enough water in your system to keep you superpowered. You should be aiming to drink at least two litres a day. Did you know that often when you feel hungry, your body is actually telling you it needs water, not food? So next time you reach for that snack-bar, go for a glass of H_2O instead!

4. DO YOU . . .

Hate fruit and vegetables?
YES ☐ **NO** ☑

You should be eating about five portions of fruit and vegetables a day. It may sound like a lot, but this is the stuff Super Kids are made of. You see, fruit and vegetables are packed full of all the vital vitamins and life-saving anti-cancer chemicals that help to boost your immune-system and keep you fighting fit and alive. After all, Super Kids can't afford to get ill!

5. DO YOU . . .

Snack between meals?
YES ☑ **NO** ☐

When was the last time you saw a superhero snacking on a doughnut! When you're busy saving the world, you need to make sure you've got enough in your tummy to keep energy levels up all day. That means proper food at breakfast, lunch and dinner – and then you'll be able to climb that tree, crush that genetically modified soya bean or save that tiger from extinction. Carbohydrates, like pasta, cereal and brown bread are great slow-burning fuels that you give you energy. Meanwhile, proteins like milk, meat, cheese or eggs make sure your body can repair all the wear and tear it gets while trying to save the world.

Five portions of fruit and vegetable per day are the perfect way to juggle an active life and a healthy diet.

6. DO YOU . . .

Pester your parents to buy the latest cool toy or game?
YES ☐ **NO** ☑

The advertisers have you clocked. They know that when you go on and on at your Mum and Dad about a toy, they will listen. Only you have the energy and perseverance to gradually erode their willpower, until they can't resist anymore and buy you that toy just to SHUT YOU UP! Well, just imagine if you used the same power to get them to buy organic food or reduce chemicals in your home? Don't use your pester power for the wrong things – use it to save the world.

7. DO YOU . . .

Spend more than three hours a day watching TV?
YES ☑ **NO** ☐   Sometimes

Telly can be really interesting, fun and informative. But telly can also be a waste of your precious time and your life. Be selective in the telly you watch. Most kids watch telly and talk about what's on with friends. Super Kids don't want to be left out, but they definitely don't want to end up as a TV Zombie!

8. DO YOU . . .

Spend most of your time sitting around indoors?
YES ☑ **NO** ☐

Are you getting your regular dose of fresh air and exercise? Being out and about, not sitting on the couch or playing computer games, is the best way to keep you mentally and physically fit – and ready to tackle the planet's needs! Aim for at least 20 minutes of outdoor exercise a day. Just dig out that bike, take the dog for a walk or get friends together for a kick-around.

Try making your own theatre – it's far
more fun than watching telly, AND you get to
make up your own stories.

9. ARE YOU . . .

A fashion victim?
YES ☐ NO ☑

Label alert! Are you always on at your parents to buy you the latest Nike trainers or designer gear? If so, you could be in danger of turning into a fashion victim. Like games and toys, clothes and shoes are cleverly advertised by big companies to trick you into believing they're a 'must-have' item. But stop and think. You've got along perfectly fine so far, without the latest pair of trainers — and there's nothing wrong with the pair you've got. Do you really need them? Or are they just to look cool?

What's more, you might not be the only victim behind your fashion label. High street stores hide a workforce of human sufferers, who stitch the tiny threads on your trendy £90 trainers, for less than the cost of a loaf of bread a day. These people are exploited by many of the big high street clothes chains, who make a fortune out of our desire for the trendiest, the coolest or the most expensive clobber. Find out which stores and brands are OK, and which are really dodgy from the Clean Clothes Campaign at www.cleanclothes.org. You can also find some funky alternatives at www.ethicaltrade.org.

10. DO YOU . . .

Think celebrities have the ideal lifestyle?
YES ☐ NO ☑

Don't get caught up in the celebrity trap. Lots of stars who seem to have everything, have experienced one of life's most tragic and stressful events — their marriages have fallen through. Think of Jennifer Aniston, Kate Winslet and J-Lo and remember being super-sleek, super-beautiful or super-rich doesn't always make you happy.

Don't waste your time trying to copy the latest celebrity look. Your David Beckham haircut will only be fashionable until he changes his style again. Be happy with your looks and who you are. People will respect you for being individual.

You can always spot a fashion victim. They're not interested in clothes at all – just the labels.

11. DO YOU . . .

Throw things away without thinking where they end up?
YES ☐ NO ☑

There's no excuse now! This book has hopefully shown you just how much damage humans are doing to the planet, by not thinking about the waste we're creating and then piling it back into landfill sites. By damaging the planet, we're only damaging ourselves. Remember, 65% of household waste can be recycled. Think before you throw that can in the bin!

12. DO YOU . . .

Ignore packaging labels on cosmetics and toiletries?
YES ☐ NO ☑

Have a look at the ingredients label on the back of your favourite deodorant. Does the list sound like the contents of a witch's spell or a recipe to kill off vampires? Is it something that you want to be smearing on your skin? Remember, that one your best weapons are the amazing eco-files stored in your eco-detective brain. So keep an eye on labels and stay informed. Then, when the papers start warning of health risks linked with one chemical or another, you'll remember where you saw that name before.

When it comes to cleaning and moisturising, always go for a natural alternative. Because it's not just your health you could be harming. Before cosmetics can be sold to humans, there are laws saying they must be tested for safety. A lot of the time, this testing is carried out on animals, and many animals may have died just so you could have the latest beauty cream. Look for the Star and Rabbit sign on products. This proves they haven't been tested on animals.

HOW DID YOU DO?

Mark a point for each YES that you ticked, then tot them all up. How many points did you score? And what does your total mean?

0-3 **NATURAL BORN SUPER KID!** You're a shining example to all wannabe Super Kids! Now it's time to start looking after the planet in the same way you look after yourself.

4-7 **A SUPER KID IN THE MAKING!** You're almost there. Super Kids' status is in sight! You just need to look at the areas you didn't score too highly on, to work out where you need to improve.

8-11 **STILL SOME WORK TO DO!** A few too many 'YES' answers here! There's quite a lot of work to do before you can call yourself a true Super Kid. Set yourself some goals, whether it's cutting down on TV, not eating sweet snacks or pestering your parents.

12 **RED ALERT!** Oh dear Super Kid. That's the full Dirty Dozen. Before you can save the world, you're going to have to save yourself!

Get out there!

Right Super Kids, it's time for you to get active and make a noise! One of the best ways to get involved in daily life is to start campaigning. Be a really proactive eco-hero and make those Zombie Adults sit up and pay attention! Here are three of the best ways to make a difference:

1. Spread the word

Rally together, Super Kids. Form an action group and think of ways to 'raise awareness'. After all, two super-brains are better than one!

If the cause you're campaigning for isn't well-known — an endangered animal species, for example — think of ways to flag it up. Making posters is a great way of catching people's attention. Put them up on school notice boards, in local community centres or ask if you can leave one in your local shop. Remember to:

! Make a bold statement

Statistics are a great way of getting your point across. Check out some of the SUPERFACTS in this book for ideas.

! Guide the Way

Suggest ways people can help, or places they can find out more. Give the details — including name, address and website — of a charity they can donate to.

2. Sign up!

It's all about people power — and petitions can really make a difference! You need to find at least 100 people who support your cause. Then write a short statement on what it's all about and get them to sign it. For example:

'The following people all wish to see animal testing banned . . .'

Once you've got enough signatures, send it to your local MP. Or if you feel very strongly, to the Prime Minister himself!

To find names and addresses of government members — including instructions on how to send direct mail to them — have a look at www.writetothem.com.

3. Dear Sir or Madam . . .

Letters can be very powerful tools. One charity called Amnesty International even gets people to write letters, to campaign for the release of political prisoners. It really can work! Match your cause with someone who can make a change and get scribbling, Super Kids! People to try include:

✐ **Your local MP** This is someone who works right in the heart of government — ideal for causes that affect the world or the nation. Ask them to raise a question in Parliament, or write to the Minister/Secretary of State for you.

✐ **Your local council** If your issue is about something closer to home, like making your area more eco-friendly, setting up a recycling scheme or saving your park from greedy construction companies, this is where to come first.

✐ **Your local newspaper** The media is a great way of telling the public about your cause. Write to the editor and ask for his or her support. They might write an article on it or even sponsor your cause. Every bit of publicity helps!

✐ **Heads of big companies** These people are often the worst eco-destroyers. They care more about making money than looking after the world. If you don't like what a company is doing, to the environment or humans, find out all you can about what they do. Look on their website to find the name of the Director or CEO. Write and tell them what you think. You could advise them you have already written to your local MP. That should make them listen!

Letter writing tips

⇒ **Always be polite**
Start with 'Dear Mr or Ms X' and finish with 'Yours sincerely.'

⇒ **Don't get angry**
Even if these people have caused the problem. You need them to help you.

⇒ **Be clear**
Explain why you are writing. Don't assume they know about the issue.

⇒ **Always put your age**
They might listen to kids more!

⇒ **Be personal**
Talk about why you got involved and why you care.

⇒ **Get the address right**
It's no good if it doesn't arrive at all!

⇒ **Include an SAE**
Then there's no excuse not to reply.

Useful people to know

HERE IS A LIST OF SOME OF THE GREAT ORGANISATIONS THAT WILL GIVE YOU MORE INFORMATION AND HELP YOU SAVE THE PLANET!

AURO ORGANIC PAINT SUPPLIES LTD
Organic paints that don't pollute the environment. ● 01799 543 077
www.auroorganic.co.uk

BARN OWL TRUST A charity dedicated to conserving the barn owl and its natural habitat in the UK. ● 01364 653 026 **www.barnowltrust.org.uk**

BAT CONSERVATION TRUST UK
An organisation devoted to the conservation of bats and their habitats. ● 020 7627 2629
www.bats.org.uk

BATTERSEA DOGS' HOME
An organisation that rescues and re-homes stray and ill-treated dogs and cats. ● 020 7622 3626
www.dogshome.org

BBC MAKES AND BAKES A website with ideas and instructions to accompany the Blue Peter TV show. ●
www.bbc.co.uk/cbbc/bluepeter/makes

BRITISH HEDGEHOG PRESERVATION SOCIETY A UK Charity dedicated to helping and protecting hedgehogs.
● 01584 890 801
www.software-technics.co.uk/bhps

BRITISH TOY MAKERS GUILD
Promotes British craft toys for children and grown-ups.
● **www.toymakersguild.co.uk**

BRITISH UNION FOR THE ABOLITION OF VIVISECTION Britain's anti-vivisection organisation that campaigns to end all animal experimentation. ● 020 7700 4888
www.buav.org

BTCV An organisation that works with volunteers to bring about positive environmental change.
● 01491 821 600 **www.btcv.org**

BUTTERFLY CONSERVATION Protects native butterflies, moths and their habitats from a range of threats.
● 0870 774 4309
www.butterfly-conservation.org.uk

BUY RECYCLED A handy guide to products available in the UK containing recycled materials.
● www.recycledproducts.org.uk

CAMPAIGN TO PROTECT RURAL ENGLAND Protects and enhances rural areas. ● 020 7891 2800
www.cpre.org.uk

CASH FOR CANS Promotes local level aluminium recycling in the UK and abroad, offering incentives to individuals and organisations.
● www.cashforcans.co.uk

CENTRE FOR ALTERNATIVE TECHNOLOGY Inspires and enables people to live more sustainably.
● 01654 705 950
www.cat.org.uk

CHILDREN'S SCRAPSTORE Recycles safe waste products to create resources for children's play activities.
● 01179 252 229
www.childrensscrapstore.com

CHOOSE CLIMATE Calculates the cost of your flight to the environment.
● www.chooseclimate.org

COMPASSION IN WORLD FARMING Campaigns to end factory farming and improve the transport of animals.
● www.ciwf.org

COMPOST ASSOCIATION Promotes good practice in composting and the use of composted materials. ● 01933 227 777 www.Compost.org.uk

COUNTRYSIDE FOUNDATION FOR EDUCATION An educational charity that works to bring the countryside into the classroom. ● 01422 885 566
www.countrysidefoundation.org.uk

EARTH CENTRE A charity that promotes sustainable living.
● 01709 513 933
www.earthcentre.org.uk

ECO-BABES Providers of real cloth nappies and organic baby goods for environmentally conscious parents.
● 01366 387 851
www.eco-babes.co.uk

THE ECOLOGIST The world's longest running environmental magazine.
● www.theecologist.org

ECOZONE An online range of eco-friendly products for use in and around the home.
● www.ecozone.co.uk

EDEN PROJECT A permanent outdoor exhibition that highlights our relationship with plants. With over 100,000 plants from all over the world. ● 01726 811 911
www.edenproject.co.uk

ENERGY SAVING TRUST Promotes sustainable and efficient use of energy. ● www.est.org.uk

ENERGY STAR Provides information on energy saving and the energy saving Star-rating.
● www.energystar.gov

ENGLISH HERITAGE Shows people why the historic buildings and landscape around them matter.
● 0870 3331181
www.farmgarden.org.uk

ENGLISH NATURE Promotes England's wildlife and natural features. ● 01733 455 101
www.english-nature.org.uk

ETHICAL CONSUMER A watchdog on the ethical status of brands.
● 0161 226 2929
www.ethicalconsumer.org

FAIRTRADE FOUNDATION Campaigns to encourage the growth of global fairtrade. ● www.fairtrade.org

FEDERATION OF CITY FARMS AND COMMUNITY GARDENS Sustainable and community-led projects, working with people, animals and plants.
● 01179 231 800
www.farmgarden.org.uk

FOOD STANDARDS AGENCY Find out about food labelling, organic food, food safety and GM crops.
● 020 7276 8000
www.foodstandards.gov.uk

FRIENDS OF THE EARTH A national environmental pressure group.
● 0207 490 1555
www.foe.co.uk

FUTURE FORESTS Help plant trees to help neutralise carbon dioxide emissions and sustain the environment for the future. ● 0870 241 1932 www.futureforests.com

GIRL GUIDES Exciting challenges and adventures for girls and young women. ● 020 7834 6242
www.girlguiding.org.uk

GLOBAL ACTION PLAN Helps people make positive changes at home, work, school and the wider community.
● 020 7405 5633
www.farmgarden.org.uk

GREEN BATTERIES Promotes the use of rechargeable batteries.
● www.greenbatteries.com

GREEN BOARD GAMES Ethical games for all ages. ● 01494 538 999 www.greenboardgames.com

GREENPEACE Campaigns to expose global environmental problems and their causes. ● 020 7188 1068
www.greenpeace.org.uk

GREEN WORKS Collects redundant office equipment for schools.
● 020 7981 0450
www.green-work.co.uk/

HENRY DOUBLEDAY RESEARCH ASSOCIATION (HDRA) Researches and promotes organic gardening, farming and food. ● 02476 303 517 www.hdra.org.uk/

H2OUSE How to use water efficiently in the home. ● www.h2ouse.org

MAN IN SEAT 61 Advice on how to travel the world by rail and sea by a man who has done it himself. ● www.seat61.com

MEDIA FAMILY Maximises the benefits, and minimises the harm of mass media on children. ● 011 888 672 5437 or 011 612 672 5437 www.mediafamily.org

NATIONAL ASSOCIATION OF FARMERS' MARKETS All about farmers' markets in the UK. ● 01225 787 914 www.farmersmarkets.net

NATIONAL ASSOCIATION OF NAPPY SERVICES Promotes and educates about the use of cotton nappies instead of disposable ones. ● 0121 693 4949 www.changeanappy.co.uk

NATIONAL PLAYING FIELDS ASSOCIATION Committed to protecting and improving playing fields. ● 0207 833 5360 www.npfa.co.uk

NATIONAL RECYCLING FORUM A guide to recycled products in the UK. ● 020 7089 2100 www.recycledproducts.org.uk

NATIONAL MARITIME MUSEUM Over 500 years of maritime history all under one roof. ● 020 8858 4422 www.nmm.ac.uk

NATIONAL TRUST Set up to protect and care for threatened coastline, countryside and buildings. ● 0870 458 4000 www.nationaltrust.org.uk

NATURAL COLLECTION An online catalogue of goods that are in complete harmony with nature. ● 0870 331 33 33 www.naturalcollection.com

NATURAL ECO TRADING Environmentally friendly household cleaning products. ● 01892 616871 www.greenbrands.co.uk

NO SWEAT Campaign against sweatshops. ● 07904 431 959 www.nosweat.org.uk

OLLIE RECYCLES A website for children to learn the 3Rs: Reduce, Reuse and Recycle. ● www.ollierecycles.com/uk

ORGANIC FOOD, UK Everything you need to know about organic food.
● www.organicfood.co.uk

OXFAM Helping to finding lasting solutions to poverty and suffering around the world. ● 0870 333 2700 www.oxfam.org.uk

PESTICIDE ACTION NETWORK UK Aims to reduce our dependence on toxic chemicals and pesticides.
● 020 7274 8895 www.pan-uk.org

PHENOLOGY NETWORK Shows how you can help record changes in nature and climate in the UK. ● 01476 581 111 www.phenology.org.uk

PLANTLIFE A national membership charity dedicated to conserving plant life in its natural habitat.
● 020 7808 0100 www.plantlife.org.uk

PUMPKIN CARVING For information on celebrating halloween and growing pumpkins.
● www.pumpkin-carving.com

RAINFOREST ACTION NETWORK Works to protect tropical rainforests and the human rights of those living in and around them. ● 0131 622 7188 www.ran.org

RAMBLERS' ASSOCIATION Working for walkers across England, Scotland and Wales. ● 020 7339 8500 www.ramblers.org.uk

RECYCLE NOW Information and helpful tips on how to best dispose of household rubbish.
● www.recyclenow.co.uk

RETHINK RUBBISH Lots of helpful advice on how to avoid throwing stuff away, that you can recycle.
● www.rethinkrubbish.com

REUZE Where, what and how to recycle in the UK.
● www.reuze.co.uk/home.shtml

ROYAL HORTICULTURAL SOCIETY The UK's leading gardening charity dedicated to advancing horticulture and promoting good gardening.
● 020 7834 4333 www.rhs.org.uk

ROYAL PARKS FOUNDATION Conserves parks so future generations can enjoy them.
● 020 7 298 2000 www.royalparks.gov.uk

RSPCA Rescues and re-homes animals suffering from distress or cruelty. ● 0870 333 5999 www.rspca.org.uk

ROYAL SOCIETY FOR THE PROTECTION OF BIRDS (RSPB) A charity working for a healthy environment, rich in birds and wildlife.
● 01767 680 551 www.rspb.org.uk

SAMARITAN'S PURSE INTERNATIONAL Send gift-filled shoe boxes to needy children around the world. ● 020 8559 2044 www.samaritanspurse.org

SAVE ENERGY How to save energy in your home. ● www.saveenergy.co.uk

SAVE OUR SEEDS (SOS) An EU-wide campaign to keep organic seeds free from genetically modified plants. ● www.saveourseeds.org

SAVE THE CHILDREN Working to create a better future for children around the world. ● 020 7703 5400 www.savethechildren.org.uk

SCHOOL GOVERNMENT PUBLISHING CO. Information about field study and environmental education centres for schools. ● www.schoolgovernment.co.uk

SCOUTS ASSOCIATION Sign up for action packed adventures with the cubs, scouts, beavers or explorers. ● 0845 300 1818 www.scouts.org.uk

STEEL CAN RECYCLING INFORMATION BUREAU (SCRIB) Find out about can-recycling in the UK. ● 01639 872626 www.scrib.org

SMALL WORLD OF TOYS AND HOBBIES Eco-friendly wooden toys and dolls' houses.● 01984 64 11 22 www.smallworldtoys.co.uk

SOIL ASSOCIATION A campaigning and certification organisation for organic food and farming. ● 0117 929 0661 www.soilassociation.org

SPRINTS / RECYCOOL A nationwide scheme enabling you to swap empty print cartridges and old mobile phones, for new school equipment. ● 0845 130 2050 www.recycool.org

SURFERS AGAINST SEWAGE (SAS) Campaigns for clean, safe recreational water in the UK, free from sewage, toxic chemicals and nuclear waste. ● 01872 553 001 www.sas.org.uk

SAFE-ROUTES-TO-SCHOOLS INFORMATION TEAM (SUSTRANS) A sustainable transport charity that campaigns for a reduction in motor traffic like cars, and their bad effects. ● 0117 926 8893 www.sustrans.org.uk

TALKING BALLOONS A website that specialises in screen-printed, biodegradable balloons for birthday parties and celebrations. ● 01246 590402 www.talking-balloons.co.uk

TREE COUNCIL Protects, plants and cares for trees and their environment. ● 020 7407 9992 www.treecouncil.org.uk

WASTE WATCH WASTELINE An organisation that promotes and encourages waste reduction, reuse and recycling. ● 020 7089 2100 **www.wastewatch.org.uk** or **www.wasteonline.org.uk**

WASTE CONNECT An online database for searching recycling points in the UK. ● 01743 343 403 **www.wasteconnect.co.uk** or **www.wastecpoint.co.uk**

WHITEDOT An organisation that campaigns to reduce the amount of telly we watch. ● **www.whitedot.org**

WIGGLY WIGGLERS Supplies wormeries, gardening accessories, and wildlife products for your garden. ● 01981 500 391 **www.wigglywigglers.co.uk**

WILDFOWL AND WETLANDS TRUST Set up to research and protect wild birds and ducks and their natural habitats. ● 01453 891 900 **www.wwt.org.uk**

THE WILDLIFE TRUSTS Everything you need to know about wildlife and our environment. ● 0870 036 7711 **www.wildlifetrusts.org.uk**

WOODCRAFT FOLK Great ways to spend your time, including games, drama, craftwork,

education and eco-holidays for young people. ● 020 8672 6031 **www.woodcraft.org.uk**

WOODLAND TRUST Working for the protection of Britain's native forests and woodlands. ● 01476 581 135 **www.woodland-trust.org.uk**

WORLD WILDLIFE FUND UK (WWF-UK) A conservation organisation, working to protect animal species and their natural habitats around the world. ● 01483 426 444 **www.wwf.org.uk**

YOUNG PEOPLES TRUST FOR THE ENVIRONMENT (YPTE) Packed with helpful information to encourage kids' understanding of the environment. ● 01483 539600 **www.yptenc.org.uk**

Raise the alarm! Spread the word!

You can help Siren make a safer world for wildlife

You've read the book, and you Super Kids are now in the know! But imagine all the people who haven't got a clue that the planet is in trouble. We need them on board – we can't do it alone – we've got to get to them fast and turn them all into planet-saving super-heroes.

Siren Conservation Education gets the message out, sounding alarm bells about the state of the planet. From badgers to lynx and lions, Siren works to inspire people to care for and protect the natural world.

Siren is working with people who literally save all sorts of animals, all over the world from all dying out. Helping creatures like the beautiful African painted dogs (above), which live in family groups and dance around like elves in the forest, or the gentle dugong sea cows tending their babies in the water like mermaids. These animals are threatened and without our help might disappear forever.

Here in the UK, Siren helps children make friends with the wildlife on their doorstep. Visit our website www.siren.org.uk. While you're there, step through the migration portals and get on the bird super-highway, where you can join the big birds as they swoop down to Africa twice a year. We can even visit your school and set up animal saving days. Or maybe you can fundraise to help us stop the mermaids or the African fairy dogs from disappearing forever?

Siren was set up by Sasha Norris, the author of this book. Check out her planet-saving activities and efforts to remain a Super Kid and avoid Zombiedom at www.sashanorris.co.uk.

THE FUTURE IS IN YOUR HANDS

THE YOUNG PEOPLE'S TRUST FOR THE ENVIRONMENT (YPTE) IS HERE TO HELP YOUNG PEOPLE FIND OUT MORE ABOUT THE NATURAL WORLD AND WHAT WE CAN DO TO HELP PROTECT IT.

We believe that everyone – young or old – can help to make a difference to our environment every day. It's in your power to do something to help, and the great news is that getting started is easy! There are so many small ways that you can help – by switching off lights when you leave a room, not leaving the tap running when you brush your teeth or maybe by recycling as much of your rubbish as possible.

Even small contributions can create change if enough people get involved. If every household in the UK replaced one 100 watt light bulb with a low energy bulb, we would save the amount of energy produced by medium sized power station during a year!

It's really important that today's young people – the future guardians of our planet – know they can help to look after it. That's why we offer a range of services specially designed for young people and teachers, but useful to anybody who wants to find out more about the natural world and how we can all help. The great news is that most of our services are free!

If you need any information about the environment or any kind

of wildlife, then www.yptenc.org.uk is a great place to start. We have hundreds of fact sheets available to print and download, and they're all free! While you're there, check out our news page – The Daily Gecko – for environmental news stories from around the world.

Plus, we also provide free environmental talks in schools, within a 100 mile radius of our two offices in Guildford, Surrey and Penrith, Cumbria. The illustrated talks focus on a range of topics, and are exciting and inspirational.

And we offer action-packed environmental courses and holidays for young people and school groups at centres in the south of England and the Lake District. They're a great way to learn more about the environment, and each course shows just how fascinating our countryside can be.

You can help us by making changes in your life to benefit the environment, and by telling your friends, parents and teachers about us. You can find details of all our services at www.yptenc.org.uk, call 01483 539600, or write to YPTE, 3 Walnut Tree Park, Walnut Tree Close, Guildford, GU1 4TR.

Come and join us!

Caithness Watch group having fun

Have a wild time

ARE YOU READY FOR SOME FUN? THEN WILDLIFE WATCH IS JUST FOR YOU!

If this book has inspired you to become an eco-warrior, (which it surely must have!) then there is just the club for you to join. Wildlife Watch has 62,000 members, and groups all around the UK where you can meet loads of other like-minded eco-warriors. As well as meeting new mates, you'll be able to put some of your new ideas for saving the planet into practice. Along the way you'll also discover more about wildlife and explore your local environment. Just some of the activities that Watch groups offer include searching for wildlife in woodlands, birdwatching, tracking animals and making casts of their footprints, pond-dipping and bat-detecting at night. Plus campaigning to save dolphins, learning from local experts and 'researching' issues in your neighbourhood. A lot of discovery is done through games and fun. You could also go out on visits to nature reserves, the seaside or even discover the wildlife of your local park.

If you feel like getting your hands dirty, you could do some conservation work, such as burning brash, raking grass, or clearing out a stream, to make better places for wildlife.

Finding out more about wildlife can give you the chance to have some unforgettable adventures. Some groups run overnight camps. One built their own shelter Ray Mears' style, using bracken, logs and fir branches. After cooking sausages, marshmallows and popcorn on the fire, they settled down to spend the night in the middle of the wood, trying not to get spooked by the rustles and calls of the wild at night!

All activities are run by registered leaders working to guidelines, so your parents can be sure you're safe, while off having adventures!

If you don't fancy being part of a group, or there isn't one near enough to

Mosaics by Melksham Watch group. There's plenty to do at Wildlife Watch!

you, there's still plenty you can do. Hundreds of members take part in Wildlife Watch's Gold Award scheme, where you can work towards your Gold Award by being awarded special badges for different activities and achievements. Every year, members of Watch receive three full-colour magazines called Watchword, packed with the latest wildlife stories and things to do. They also get three issues of Wildlife Extra, a newsletter that folds out into a fantastic poster, bursting with ideas and activities.

You can subscribe to be a member of Wildlife Watch, with your local Wildlife Trust. In most parts of the UK you can join as an individual or with your family. It won't cost more than £15 for up to four children at one address.

For details on how to join:

Visit our website at www.wildlifewatch.org.uk
Email us at Watch@wildlife-trusts.cix.co.uk
Phone us on 01636 677711
or write to us at Wildlife Watch, The Kiln, Mather Road, Newark NG24 1WT.
Or simply contact your local Wildlife Trust, which looks after your Watch membership.

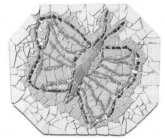

SUPER KIDS

is supported by

NORWICH UNION
an AVIVA company

Well Super Kids, we hope you've enjoyed this book and are inspired to do your bit to save the planet.

Norwich Union is part of Aviva plc. We are the largest insurer in the UK and the largest life and pensions provider in Europe. Through our business we help our customers to take care of what's important to them, like their house, car, health, future and much, much more.

We believe that it's right to look after what's important, and what could be more important than ensuring our planet is taken care of? That's why we've chosen to support this book.

Here are some of the ways that Norwich Union is working to reduce our impact on the environment:

☑ All electricity used in Norwich Union buildings now comes from renewable energy sources like wind or solar power. We are always trying to reduce our consumption further by switching off lights and computers when we are not using them, and turning the heating down if it gets too warm.

☑ We try and communicate with other people electronically as much as possible, which reduces the amount of paper we use. Last year we used paper that was equivalent to 980 football pitches of trees. The paper we do use comes from trees in sustainable forests where three trees are planted for each one that is cut down.

Cans – 96%

Cardboard – 95%

Waste Paper – 100% or 156 football pitches of trees

Toner cartridges – 95%

Plastic cups – 65%

Computers and other IT waste – 96%

We encourage our employees to recycle materials where possible. There's still some work to be done, but in 2004 we managed to recycle what you see on this list.

We also recycle mobile phones, light bulbs, CDs, batteries and carpets. And we even have a wormery at our head office in London where the worms eat all the food scraps from our canteen.

Just as you will try to persuade your parents and others to help you in your goal to save the planet, we try to use our influence to encourage our suppliers and companies we have invested in to take care of the environment. We can do this because we invest over £240,000,000,000 in other companies!

Norwich Union sends you its very best wishes as you embark on your efforts to save the planet.

Keep on THINKing

The people at Think Books, who put together Super Kids, are part of Think Publishing, the country's leading environmental publisher.

Think publishes books and magazines for several organisations that will help you in your quest to become a true **Super Kid**. Why not visit their websites and find out more about them? Not all adults are Zombies, after all.

BTCV Supporting volunteering opportunities throughout the UK and across the globe. www.btcv.org

Butterfly Conservation Saving butterflies, moths and their habitats. **www.butterfly-conservation.org.uk**

CPRE For the protection and enhancement of rural England. www.cpre.org.uk

The Ramblers' Association Britain's biggest walking organisation. **www.ramblers.org.uk**

The Soil Association Campaigns for organic food, organic farming and sustainable forestry. www.soilassociation.org

The Wildfowl & Wetlands Trust The conservation of wetlands, focusing on wetland birds. **www.wwt.org.u**k

The Wildlife Trusts The UK's leading conservation charity, exclusively dedicated to wildlife. www.wildlifetrusts.org

www.thinkpublishing.co.uk

The certificate of SHAME

Well done, Super Kids. You've taken the first steps towards saving the planet. You're a true eco-hero.

But there's still one more job that needs tackling. Someone needs to tell the Zombie Adults where they're going wrong. And that someone, Super Kids, is you.

It's no good reading this book and improving the world, if the adults just hang around in the background and mess it all up again.

So here's what you do. Every time you spot one of your parents, or a teacher, or any other adult making a mess of the planet in the ways you've just been reading about, put a black mark against their name on the chart below. The first one to get five black marks pays the ultimate penalty – they have to receive THE CERTIFICATE OF SHAME!

Simply record their crimes on the certificate on the next page, write both your names on it, cut it out and present it to them. AND MAKE THEM PROMISE TO HANG IT ON THEIR WALL UNTIL THEY IMPROVE THEIR BEHAVIOUR! That should teach them a lesson they deserve.

Black marks = ✗	1	2	3	4	5
Your Mum					
Your Dad					
Your teacher					
Another Zombie adult					

I,
_____

[Your name]

hereby confirm that

_____

[The Zombie Adult's name]

has committed the following crimes against the environment, and must hang this certificate on their wall until they amend their ways and promise to stop being such a naughty adult.

Crime 1 _____

Crime 2 _____

Crime 3 _____

Crime 4 _____

Crime 5 _____